ART

for Young America

Fifth Edition

CARL J. HEYNE
Pittsburgh School System

With
FLORENCE W. NICHOLAS
MARGARET M. LEE
MABEL B. TRILLING

CHAS. A. BENNETT CO., INC.
Peoria, Illinois

154241

Library of Congress Cat. No. 60-6617
Printed in the United States of America
RM 10 9 8 7 6 5 4 3 2 1

● List of Color Illustrations

Preface...

The fifth edition of ART FOR YOUNG AMERICA is based on the same philosophy of art education as that which inspired the original effort to provide simple and enjoyable art experiences for young people. It is designed for use by all students so that they may participate in the art and beauty of the world about them. Accordingly, emphasis is placed upon experiences which will foster appreciation.

Believing that art in its many forms of expression is important to all people, the authors have endeavored to select subject matter which will appeal especially to the younger teen-age group. Materials for study cover a wide scope, ranging from the familiar things of everyday life to the masterpieces of the past and present. No attempt has been made to organize these subjects in terms of historical sequence. We leave that to a later time when students take up a detailed course in history of art.

Beginning high school students are eager and ready to explore the beauty of the world as they encounter it in nature and in various man-made art forms. They are also interested in finding out what it is that makes some things more beautiful than others. This leads easily into a study of art principles, but only nominal attention is given to these well known rules which often dominate the art course of study.

It is important for the student at the early adolescent period to begin to discover beauty in his own environment. Comparison of old and new planes as presented in Chapter 2 helps him to discover why he finds the airplane beautiful. He discovers this *for himself,* and more or less consciously he begins to think in terms of art quality.

Genuine appreciation cannot be imposed or "learned" like the multiplication table. We cannot induce esthetic experience by telling students that they *should* feel pleasurable responses. Psychologists tell us that the esthetic experience is due to a responsive attitude of mind in which *the pleasure tone is dominant.*

Obviously we must pursue other methods of procedure than those which are successful in such subjects as mathematics or science. To insist that our young people must like our selections of the "best kinds of art" is futile and may easily result in a type of pseudo-appreciation which would be most unfortunate. Whatever feeling a student will have for art, let it be genuine— and let it be his own, based on a study of values from his experiences.

C.J.H.

Table of Contents

Chapter One | **Art Is for You**

Inside all of us there is a hunger for beauty in our lives. Whether we realize it or not, all of us wish for sights upon which we may "feast our eyes" and thus satisfy our "hunger." Psychologists tell us that we are born with this desire, so it is quite natural for each of us to look for and appreciate beautiful things.

The mechanical device pictured on page 7 is known as the Solar Toy. It serves no purpose except to amuse and entertain. When the sun comes up, the toy begins to spin, dip, and whirl in a circus of breathtaking color and dazzling motion. It is powered only by solar energy. At the touch of a sunbeam, the lightweight aluminum parts glide into their dizzy, swirling dance. Motors turn, wheels revolve, pistons rise and fall, and all the hues of the rainbow flash in the sunlight. At sun-

down all movement and sound cease, for the toy operates only by the light of the sun—the brighter the better.

Charles Eames, famous designer and architect, created this abstract design of aluminum. It was part of an experiment to find new uses for this metal.

When we encounter something as delightful as the Solar Toy, we respond at once with pleasure. Many things in the world can arouse this feeling—a flaming sunset; strong-muscled horses with flying manes and tails; a jet plane high above the earth, leaving behind its vapor trails that disappear in the distance; a powerful rocket hurtling into orbit; or a church spire reaching upward.

Enjoyment of beauty does not always depend upon such dramatic sights as those mentioned above. There are many features of everyday life that

6

Solar Toy.

contribute to your enjoyment of beauty, though you may not notice some of them until you begin your study here. The lustrous surface and pleasing contours of a modern utensil may catch your attention in the kitchen. You may discover that the rich upholstery fabric on a living room chair looks very handsome against the softer color of the wall. Outside the house you may notice the pattern of tree branches against the sky, or brightly colored flowers afire with the sun. All day long you may see displays of beauty at home, at school, and all around—that is, if your eyes are educated to see them, and if you have the inclination to enjoy them.

Some people seem to have a habit of mind which causes them to notice chiefly the things they don't like, and to express their feelings freely! This certainly does not endear them to their friends; most important of all, such a super-critical way of thinking prevents them from enjoying many worthwhile things.

Instead of saying, "I hate that color," or, "I can't stand that picture," it is better to look carefully at colors and forms, then try to select those that you *do* like. Perhaps you will eventually learn to like all colors, and many new forms, although you will always have favorites.

Nature Provides for Enjoyment of Beauty

Everyone enjoys the displays of beauty that nature presents—the sun rising, red and gold, above a blue Northern lake; the rugged snow-capped Rockies; the brilliant colors of autumn leaves in the Adirondacks; a far-reaching field of bluebonnets in Texas; a road through the pine forests of Washington; the Grand Canyon in Arizona; a view of the sea beyond California beaches; or the picturesque Maine coast. People take long trips to see such sights as these, and come home with lasting memories. These experiences help to satisfy the need within all of us to enjoy beauty.

Probably you cannot now take long trips across the country to see the most spectacular sights, but you need not lack for beauty in your life. Every locality has attractive streets, parks, and other beauty spots. A small garden with a few simple flowers can be a place of bright beauty. Even a vegetable garden contains attractive plants—for example, a head of cabbage with its curly, cup-shaped leaves, or bright red tomatoes partly hidden by emerald green.

The study of beauty in animal forms is fascinating. It's fun to compare the lines and contours of different breeds of dogs and to think of words which describe them.

For instance, what dogs do you know that have long, flowing lines and slender proportions? Which ones have short, well-rounded curves and almost square proportions? Recall if you can the different kinds of horses you have seen—from the sleek, long-legged racer to the powerful little mustang.

8

It is interesting to see shapes and lines in the feline family—the lion, tiger, panther, and our domestic cat.

This kind of study will help you to observe more closely and to discover beauty where you had never before noticed it.

Art Qualities in Man-Made Products

Our twentieth-century world is filled with thousands of small, machine-made articles that were unknown a century or so ago, and here too we can find beauty. Designers combine structural improvements and eye-appeal to please prospective buyers. The same is true of automatic refrigerators and other large appliances. But no one would wish to buy a household appliance only for its looks. Industrial engineers and designers must be sure that the mechanical design of household appliances results in efficient operation. Functional efficiency and art quality are as important when selecting household appliances or furnishings as when buying a house or an automobile.

Suppose that you wish to buy a new chair for the living room. Naturally, you want it to have pleasing lines and to be upholstered in a fabric that goes well with the other colors in the room. These things you can test with your eye, but what about functional quality? It is important to know whether the chair will wear well and be comfortable to sit in, yet many people buy chairs and sofas without investigating wear and trying them out for comfort. Other functional qualities include the weight of the chair and the durability and "cleanability" of the fabric. A chair that requires two people to move it out from the wall on cleaning day, or one which is covered with a hard-to-clean fabric, can become a nuisance.

Think well about the functional nature of any article which you expect to be useful as well as pleasing to the eye. For example, what would you want in the design of a car besides good lines and color? Think of head room, comfortable seats, mechanical features, and other points. Remember that appearance and function are both important in a good car.

Enjoyment of Sculpture, Painting, and Architecture

Besides appreciating beauty as it occurs in nature and in the articles of everyday life, you can get much pleasure from works of art from the past and present. A lifetime can be spent in the study of any one form of great art expression. However, you can easily become acquainted with examples of fine painting, sculpture, and famous buildings. In later chapters you will find pictures and information helpful to your understanding and enjoyment of these works of art. Originals of many paintings shown in this book are on public display. In your future travels, or even in your own community, you may be able to visit art galleries and shows where you can see the originals.

Some of the sculptures are also in art galleries, and many others are located in parks and memorial plots. Famous buildings can also be visited; often it is possible—and interesting—to go inside as well as to view them from outside.

Your interest and appreciation will be increased when you learn how and why art works were created.

Do You Want Art in Your Home?

To some people this question may mean only pictures on the walls and statues on the mantelpiece. These people mistake the real meaning of the question. A home may possess many art qualities and not have a single picture or statue in it.

Art in your home means attractive outside appearance and surroundings; rooms that are convenient and inviting; the best planning of walls, windows, and entrances; furniture that is serviceable and well-proportioned; effective lighting; rugs, draperies, and upholstery that please you; wisely selected china and silver; a total appearance that gives visual pleasure; and above all, good taste, regardless of what you can afford or are able to create. Then everything must be arranged pleasingly—furniture, curtains, "traffic" lanes, ornaments, and utensils. Isn't this a real challenge?

Everyone desires an attractive home. It requires study and deliberate planning. First you should learn about colors, backgrounds, proportions. Then use what you learn so that you can make your home more enjoyable.

The study of art will help you now and in the future. Now, for instance, you can make your room at home more interesting, more attractive. A certain brother and sister who planned and finished a recreation room in an unused upstairs area of their home made a big success of it because they had learned about color and design at school. The room includes orange and gray-blue painted furniture, draperies and furniture coverings of a lively patterned fabric, rag rugs, and a large game box for storage. All the friends of these young people admire the room and enjoy using it; it reflects their spirit.

Art Is for You

Anyone with eyes to see can find pleasure in the beauty of nature and in the art of man. Experiences in art appreciation are really a search for beauty, so think of them in terms of personal enrichment. Don't be disturbed if you seem to lack talent in drawing and painting. Enjoying art or beauty in things around us does not depend on special ability.

Your study of this book will help you attain high standards of good taste in various aspects of daily living—especially in such matters as selecting and arranging home furnishings, and in planning your own room and personal dress. You might become an unusually good artist in one of these activities. Indeed, art is for you!

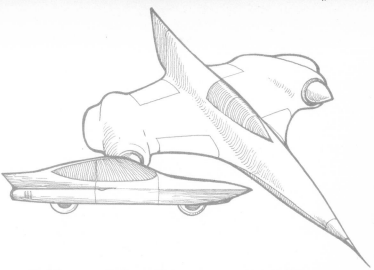

Chapter Two | Automobiles, Airplanes and Art

Have you ever seen a car that was built fifty years ago? That would be a very old car, yet automobiles were built even before that. The first ones looked more like carriages or buggies than self-powered machines, which is what the word "automobile" means.

Millions of automobiles have been built since the first ones appeared. The pictures on pages 12 and 13 show how the cars have changed from the early styles to the very different designs of the present.

The top picture on page 12 shows a car which was built in 1908. You will see that this car had no cover to protect the driver and his passengers from rain or the hot sun. This was a fair-weather car, with plush-covered seats and shiny brass ornaments. At first sign of rain the owner had to hurry his expensive auto under a roof! This car is built up of individual, boxlike sections. Notice also how high it sits above the ground.

As mentioned above, it looks more like a buggy than an automobile. But early designers had nothing to model from but buggies.

The middle picture on page 12 shows a car which was produced in 1914. Many more of these were built than of the 1908 model. This one has side doors and includes a top which was used in bad weather. You can see that this 1914 model changed considerably from the 1908 car. It no longer resembled a buggy, but was built as a single unit. Its proportions were longer and lower, but it was no sport model by today's standards!

The 1931 model, at the bottom of page 12, shows further improvements over the first model we examined. Notice the smoother blending of body sections. Also, the curved back was an innovation. Hinged at the bottom, it became a storage unit or "trunk" which replaced the strapped-on auto trunks

*These three cars show the development in automobile design. (Top) A 1908
model resembles the horse-drawn carriage, but without a top. (Center) A 1914
model with lower, longer proportions. (Bottom) A 1931 model with more
pleasing lines and proportions.*

PONTIAC MOTOR DIVISION, GENERAL MOTORS CORPORATION

that early car owners used when traveling. The "trunk" of this model, however, included an extra space for passengers, called a rumble seat. Riders in a rumble seat always had fresh air, and sometimes a good drenching too! As you know, today's convertible cars are designed so that all passengers ride inside, and the "trunk" is used not only for carrying luggage but on some models may also store a roll-back top.

Even though the 1931 car was an improvement over the other two, all three still had several things in common. They all sit high off the ground. This is because the wheels are large, and the body doesn't fit down between them. Instead it sits perched up on the axles. The fenders, lights, bumpers, horns, even the spare tires, appear to be tacked on rather than designed as parts of the body. This is because they were added for convenience, rather than planned from the beginning.

What a difference there is in the 1967 car! The entire body and all its

attached parts are designed as a unit, with each part fitting smoothly to the next. In fact, you can't see where one section joins another. This is because the designers thought of the car as one piece, not as several pieces put together, such as in the older models.

Now compare the lines of the cars. In the old cars the curves are short and not well related to the other lines. The fenders were bolted to the outside of the body for a purely functional reason; that is, because they were necessary. Without these fenders the tires would throw up water and mud from the road. The new car has fenders too, but notice the improved design. These fenders are hidden wells under the outside edges of the body, permitting a smooth, unbroken surface from front to rear. Notice especially the subtle shadow line from the headlight to the tip of the rear fender, and also the single, clean decorative strip which leads the eye swiftly from front to rear. The lines of the fenders and running

13

boards of the old models seem awkward by comparison.

A study of the windshield and roof of the new model shows how they blend with the shape and structure of the car. This was not true of the old models.

The design of the later model flows in long, unbroken lines and fine curves from front to back. The shorter lines blend with the long ones, helping to create the impression of quiet, smooth speed combined with elegance.

Perhaps you like antique cars. They are fun to look at and drive. But they were styled for another day and do not provide the speed and smoothness required by today's travelers.

Repetition Is Rhythm— A Principle of Art

Everyone knows what is meant by rhythm in music. There are waltz rhythms, march rhythms, and others. Music carries us along by a succession of sounds *repeated* in rhythm. The rhythm is the pattern or design of the repeated sounds. When we look at a painting, a new skyscraper, or the front grille of a new car, we also feel a kind of rhythm. Our eyes follow lines and forms that are *repeated* to produce a rhythm. In good design there are many repetitions of the same lines and forms. In a skyscraper, for example, the vertical lines of windows may be emphasized throughout the building. This creates a pattern or rhythm of vertical lines. The grille on a car may be a series of horizontal lines and small open spaces, repeated over and over. This too is rhythm. So when you think of rhythm, think of repetition—of pattern, of lines, of forms.

The 1967 car on page 17 provides an example of art rhythm. A series of horizontal lines, leading from front to rear, creates a feeling of speed. We see this even while the car is standing still. These long, unbroken lines were for a time called "streamlining," and were at first considered quite an innovation. But streamlines were new only to automobiles and other industrial designs, not to the world of nature. Among dogs, the greyhound and whippet are "streamlined models." Their long, slim bodies, tapered heads, and slender legs combine to produce a shape that suggests swift movement.

Streamlining Suggests Speed

The eye can move rapidly from front to rear of a streamlined object, without interruption. Even when there is no real movement of the object, the impression is that of speed. Certainly this kind of design is well chosen for the modern car. Even trucks are now streamlined. Airplanes, trains, and boats offer other examples of streamlining in modern industrial design. In all these cases speed is desirable, and a flowing movement in the design helps to create the impression of swift movement.

Good Proportions Help

It is not only clean line and smooth form that make the modern automobile better looking than that of forty or fifty years ago. The modern car is more attractive because its proportions are better. The hood, body, and rear deck of the newer model fit into a single, long, low rectangle. The older model is shorter in proportion to its height, and stands high off the ground.

In a vehicle that speeds over smooth roads, these are important design elements. The longer, lower car with its smooth surfaces gives less resistance as well as an impression of power and speed. It is less likely to tip over, and holds the road better. We feel safer in a lower car. We sacrifice ease of getting in and out for the comforts of riding in a long, wide, low-centered automobile.

Beauty of design depends to considerable extent upon pleasing proportions and well-planned relation of spaces. It's fun to look at automobiles and try to see them in terms of proportions. Look for small divisions of spaces as well as large ones. Can you find forms that are large, yet designed to be inconspicuous? Notice the roof and windows of the 1967 car. For good appearance they are meant to be fairly inconspicuous compared with the mass of the body. Also, being relatively small they are lightweight. This helps to keep the bulk of the car's weight close to the road for a better ride and also helps prevent turning over or swaying at safe driving speeds. To achieve this lightweight roof design, glass areas were made large, glass frames almost eliminated, and roof supports kept small and thin. Thus the long, low look is not disturbed, and the car has a clean, uncluttered appearance.

The importance of good proportion in design was known to the world long before the automobile was invented. Even the buggy was beautifully proportioned for its purpose. More than 2,000 years ago the Greeks designed a building with such near-perfect proportions that architects say it is the most beautiful building ever built. In a later chapter you'll learn more about this famous building.

From Paper to Steel

Your family car is the result of combined effort by many engineers and designers. On the drawing board and sketch pad the designer first brings form to a new car; once a design has been accepted for production, designers and engineers work together to solve technical problems. We must give credit to these designers for producing some of the handsomest products of our modern industrial world. They are really artists but, instead of brush and paint, they use steel, glass, and other materials required in the automobile. This is an excellent example of how beauty and function may be united. The modern car has been made more attractive to look at and more comfortable to drive and ride in because these artists have learned to combine beauty with the satisfaction of man's need for better transportation.

15

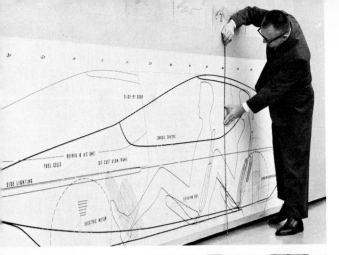

The evolution of a car from drawing board to final assembly is a fascinating study. The photographs on this page show only a few of the many steps involved in planning and executing a design for a new car. Drawings in full scale, clay models, and careful coordination or anticipation of all phases of production by the head designer contribute to the beautiful cars we see today. Remember that it's the artist-designer who is first responsible for the car's final appearance. He must guide the design from paper to steel.

Of course, some modern automobiles are designed better than others. In some, the proportions are pleasing, the curves smoother. In some the decoration is good, designed as part of the car; in others it is overdone or misplaced. As you learn more about design, you'll be able to note these differences and better appreciate qualities in automobile styling. It is closely associated with all other industrial design and with the principles of "fine art."

PONTIAC MOTOR DIVISION, GENERAL MOTORS CORPORATION

Parts Make the Whole

When we see a well designed car, we see it as a complete unit, each part belonging and blending into the total. But we know that each part required individual handling to achieve this effect. Bumpers, wheels, side panels, grilles, lights, and other parts, large and small, are carefully modeled and fitted to the overall design. The end result is a beautiful whole, simple in line but elegant in richness of form and color.

16

The photographs on this page show the individual parts of a late-model car, and the assembled model at the bottom. These parts fit together to produce a beautiful automobile. They do indeed make the whole.

You have had many opportunities to observe recent models of cars. In view of our discussion, which of the newer models do you consider especially well designed? Which one would you choose as the best? What are the reasons for your choice?

Automobile of the Future

Automobile design of the future will differ from that of the present. Imported cars have had an effect on American styling. Weight and fuel economy are important, both in driving ease and the lighter demand on the family budget. Many car manufacturers include lighter models in their lines.

In the future, engineers will improve mechanical features, and designers will make use of new methods and materials for further improvements in the appearance of the family car. But no matter how remarkable an improvement may be, something better will follow soon after. And of course everyone

PONTIAC MOTOR DIVISION, GENERAL MOTORS CORPORATION

will continue to purchase the latest model he can afford!

The two autos pictured on page 19 are experimental models designed by General Motors. The blue Runabout may someday be used to do the family shopping or take short trips in and around the city. It would be an ideal second car for driving to work, too, since it would be very easy to maneuver in traffic and to park. Imagine how simple it would be to park a car whose front wheel could be turned in a full 180 degree arc!

This model has an upper and a lower cargo area. The rear panel is hinged to provide easy access to the upper one. Two shopping carts, like the one shown behind the car, are stored in the lower one. The wheels of the cart fold back automatically when it is rolled into the car. This locks the cart in place. Head-lamps, turn signals, and parking lights are all included in the bar of lamps that runs across the front of the car, just under the hood.

The second model, the Firebird IV, is the latest in a series of General Motors' experimental cars. Earlier Firebirds were the first models in the United States to demonstrate gas tur-bine power and electronic guidance systems.

In manual operation, the driver would steer the Firebird with hand grips in the arm rests of his seat. On an automatic highway, he would turn the controls over to the electronic system which would select the proper speed, steer the car, and maintain a safe dis-tance from other cars.

The engineering and electronic in-novations built into these two autos have an important relationship with art. As you have learned, the artist or automobile stylist must make his de-sign to suit the function of the car.

In the Runabout, large window areas and compactness were his chief goals. The smooth teardrop shape with un-cluttered surfaces emphasizes compact-ness and makes cleaning and mainten-ance an easier task.

The Firebird, on the other hand, is a traveling car, built for high speed and comfort. The artist's problems included not only good visibility, but the design of fins to keep the car steady at high speeds, and exhausts for burned gases coming from the turbine. This car has a low center of gravity, and its roof is only four feet above the ground. Cut-ting down wind resistance was of great importance, since wind drag at high speed can cause vibration, noise, and serious steering problems. Like a jet plane, this car's overall body design is entirely streamlined. Explain why streamlining is so important in the de-sign of the Firebird.

Beauty in Modern Airplanes

The change in the design of air-planes since the first models is even more dramatic than with automobiles. Compare the old "flying machine" and the modern airplane, pictured on page 20. The contrast is startling! The power

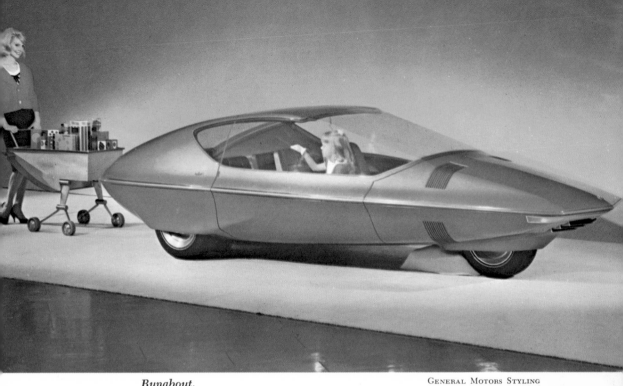

Runabout.

Firebird IV.

Curtiss pusher plane made in 1909. The design is characterized by clumsy proportions and awkward lines.

The strong lines and smooth shape of the modern plane have no resemblance to the early "crates."

20

and beauty of the modern plane are impressive, while the clumsiness of the older machine causes us to wonder that it could even get off the ground. We have only to look at the design of this old plane to understand why pilots referred to their machines as "crates."

The great beauty of the modern airplane depends partly on its strong, clean lines and smooth surfaces. Long, forceful curves sweep from nose to tail and from tip to tip of the swept-back wings. The whole design is one of power and speed, clearly expressing the purpose and function of the plane.

Perhaps the main source of beauty in the modern plane is the simplicity of its design. It is truly a product of function. The task it must perform dictates its shape and proportions. Altogether it is a beautiful arrangement of shapes and spaces, and its size is awe-inspiring, especially when we stand close by!

The older plane was interesting to look at, but its ability to fly was always a question. Improvement in the appearance of airplanes has been brought about because engineers were chiefly interested in designing machines that were safer, could fly better, and carry more passengers and freight. Changes in mechanical features of planes were accompanied by changes in appearance too. As planes became more powerful, more reliable, and more speedy, they also became more beautiful.

Anyone who has visited an airport and watched a jet transport approach the runway and land, or take off with a mighty roar of engines, knows that these are exciting and dramatic moments. The sleek beauty of these planes and their overwhelming size add to the thrill of watching them land and take off. Imagine for a moment how you would feel if instead of the great streamlined plane you expected to ride in, a "crate" like the old Curtiss pusher airplane dropped from the skies!

Art and Machines

Some people feel that real beauty is found only in the hand-painted picture or the hand-sculptured object. However, you have seen true beauty in machine-made products. Indeed, automobiles and airplanes are not only made by machines but are actually machines in themselves. There is beauty in many machines and mechanized conveyances or devices. You will find it in a train or a telephone, a boat or kitchen mixer.

A summary of the points discussed in this chapter should help reinforce your analysis of beauty in modern automobiles, airplanes, and other machines.

1. Clean, flowing lines and smooth, unified forms add to the effect of speed, strength, and power.

2. Interesting, appropriate proportions help to produce beauty of design in automobiles, airplanes, and other mechanized conveyances and devices.

3. A smooth transition from one line to another and one form to another adds to the attractiveness of the final product.

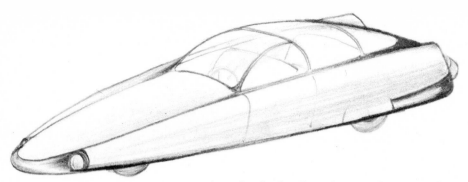

A student's drawing of a family car of the future.

4. Modern automobile and airplane designs are the result of applying principles of good design to meet engineering requirements.

5. Some designs are better than others. You should learn to recognize and enjoy the best examples of design in man-made products.

Suggestions for Activities

You will find two different types of activities at the end of each chapter in this book. For those who like to draw, there is the type of problem which requires drawing and designing. These are called Creative Activities. Besides these technical activities, there is the kind of problem which requires little or no designing. These activities are called Experiences in Appreciation. Your teacher will help you to decide when or if you should attempt each type of problem. Perhaps you will wish to try others "on your own."

Experiences in Appreciation

1. Collect pictures of automobiles. From these choose the ones that best express these good characteristics: smooth, clean lines and unbroken surfaces; speed, as shown by what we called "streamlining"; function, built to do a job first of all. Also find an example of poor automobile design. This should be easy to recognize. Give your reasons for each choice. See if you can find a single design with all of the good characteristics listed above.

2. Collect a few good examples of transition of line and form. This is seen in the way tree branches grow from the trunk, or the way in which a handle joins a cup. Look for examples of smooth transition.

3. Study repetition in art forms. You'll recall that repetition creates rhythm. How does it help to bring examples of this art principle to your attention in nature and in industrial products? Where have you noticed repeated patterns?

4. What does the word proportion mean to you? Can you define it in terms of something you have seen, something that is better because of its proper use?

5. Clip airplane pictures from mag-

The "dream" car design pictured at right was made by a professional designer for Oldsmobile. Drawings for cars of the future provide the innovations in auto styles. Designers go all-out for better appearance and more comfort.

azines and travel literature. Look for those qualities that are closely associated with aircraft: long, curved lines; smooth, strong surfaces; a sensation of great speed and power. Do you recall what requirements influenced aircraft design most? Keep these in mind as you make notes on your collection.

6. Arrange an exhibit of model planes for your classroom. If some of your classmates have flying models, you may be permitted to arrange a test flight. What characteristics do all planes have in common?

CREATIVE ACTIVITIES

1. An imaginative problem: Design the exterior of the automobile of tomorrow. Use a side view, perspective view, or any view that you can do best. Remember what you have learned about good proportions and clean, uncluttered surfaces.

2. Design a plane of tomorrow.

3. Try some imaginative drawings from new and unusual points of view. For example:

a. Draw your auto of the future in the city of the future, or a part of it. You might include other kinds of vehicles in your picture.

b. Make a picture of an airport. Why not include the terminal building as well as a plane of your own design?

4. You might have ideas for future spacecrafts, trains, ocean liners, trucks, or buses. If so, try out the principles you have learned by designing any kind of vehicle that stirs your imagination. Boys might want to try machine-part designs.

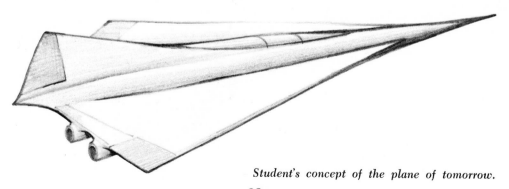

Student's concept of the plane of tomorrow.

23

Beauty in the Beast

Which animal do you think is the most beautiful? This question may be difficult for you to answer, if you are not in the habit of looking for beauty in animal forms. In answering it, many people think first of the animal which they like best. If the horse is your favorite, you may say that it is the most beautiful. If you like cats, you may say that they are the most pleasing to the eye. Either choice is good, provided you are thinking of the beauty of the animal and not of the lovable qualities that make it your favorite pet.

In this chapter we are going to think of animals in terms of art study. You will find it interesting to see how beauty in an animal is similar to beauty in a car or an airplane.

Why Are Some Animals More Beautiful Than Others?

Good design in automobiles and airplanes depends to a large extent upon clean, flowing lines and fine propor-

tions. These qualities are also very important to beauty in animal forms. Automobiles and airplanes are designed by man; animal forms are "designed" by nature. Occasionally both designers make mistakes; lines are ugly and proportions awkward. At other times both these designers do fine jobs; lines are graceful and proportions pleasing. It's fun to study animal forms for these qualities, and to discover the very fine designs that nature has created. There are other qualities besides clean line and fine proportion which are important to beauty in an animal. Color and texture of the fur or hair may contribute to its good appearance. Movement is another source of animal beauty. Some animals are graceful, others clumsy and awkward.

Beauty in the Dog Family

The dogs shown on page 25 are German shepherds. They are often called

The light and dark coloring of these dogs creates an interesting pattern against the middle grey background. If the dogs had been middle grey like the background, they would not have shown up well in the picture. When you take snapshots with your own camera, always think about the background, and plan so that your subject will stand out clearly.

"police dogs," but this is the wrong name unless they are used for police work.

German shepherds, famous for their intelligence and feats of courage, are handsome animals. Notice the proportions of the pair in the photo—strong necks and heavy shoulders, deep chests and sturdy legs, pointed ears and strong jaws, expressing strength, alertness, and dependability.

There are dozens of kinds and breeds of dogs, and they are of many shapes and sizes—tiny, huge, shaggy, smooth coated, long legged, short legged, pointed eared, droop eared, and with all sorts of tails.

Since dogs vary so much in appearance, some naturally have more beauty than others. By studying dogs in terms of design and art quality you will discover *why* one dog looks better than another. In this way you can increase the pleasure you take at the sight of a handsome boxer dog strutting down the street. Of course this need not affect the warm, happy feeling you have when your own dog comes running to meet

THE ACKLESONS

PHOTOGRAPH BY LEONARD LEE RUE III

you. It is not necessary to own beauty in order to enjoy it. Love and admiration are two different things.

In many parts of the world man has long depended upon dogs for his livelihood. Most were used for personal protection, to give warning of intruders, or to hunt. A number of breeds are still used as hunters—keen-nosed hounds for tracking; pointers and setters for locating birds; swift, long-legged hounds for running down larger game.

The long-haired dog pictured on page 26 is an Afghan. This breed of hound has been used for hundreds of years for hunting antelope and gazelles on the plains of rugged Afghanistan. Its lean body is covered with fine, silky hair that protects it against the cold. Strong shoulders, a deep chest, and powerful hind legs allow the Afghan to run long distances at great speed. Among the long-haired dogs, the Afghan is one of the most beautiful.

27

28

Bronze panther by Giuseppe Moretti. Four of these statues are mounted at the corners of a bridge crossing Panther Hollow in Schenley Park, Pittsburgh, Pennsylvania.

His proud bearing and intelligence make him a prize show dog as well as companion and hunter. The dog pictured here is "Cal," whose full name is Calah Kadesh. He is a close companion to a boy your age.

Start a collection of dog pictures. Arrange the pictures on a bulletin board and discuss the different types of lines and proportions. Look for long, streamlined effects and slender proportions, for rounded curves and heavy proportions. Try to find "dog designs" which express dignity and nobility, graceful movement, strength and courage, fun and mischief, and other ideas.

Besides dogs, the canine family includes certain wild animals such as the fox, the wolf, and the jackal. The fox is considered a rare beauty. He is small, graceful, and has a magnificent fur coat and tail, or brush. The photo of the red fox on page 27 is an accurate portrait of this beautiful animal. The fox has a reputation for being quick and cunning. There are many stories telling how he has escaped from the hunters on his trail. His beauty and personality are well expressed in the painting on page 28. The Japanese artist, Mori Ippo, used a minimum of brush strokes to create the princely, graceful effect. The lines of the grasses echo the curves of body and tail. The sly, scheming character we attribute to the animal is emphasized in the drawing of the head. If you visit Boston, you can see the original of this painting, "The White Fox," in the Museum of Fine Arts.

The Cat Family

Lions, tigers, panthers, and our own pet cats belong to a family that is

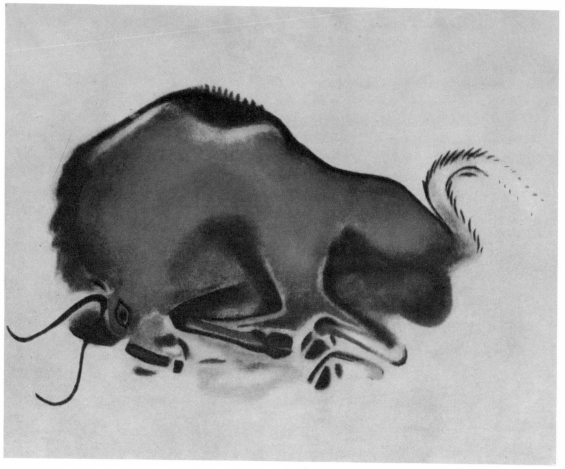

famous for its smooth grace and swift movement. "Quick as a cat" is an old saying. In the panther form shown on page 29, you can see beauty in the strong muscles. It is easy to imagine those hair-trigger muscles sliding under his skin as he leaps through space onto his prey.

The tiger has the same long, graceful lines as the panther, though his body is heavier in its proportions. It is easy to see that he belongs to the feline family. Anyone watching a tiger pace back and forth in his cage must be impressed by his restless grace and power.

Our own pet cats resemble the tiger even though many are marked differently. Indeed, they have been called "the tiger in the house." The watchful expression of the cat shown on page 30 reminds us of his much larger cousin, as he contemplates his next meal.

31

Beauty in the Wild

Some animals have certain physical characteristics which enable them to survive in the wild. Wolves, deer, and buffalo are among the wild animals still found in our nation, although the buffalo and the wolf are far fewer than when the first settlers encountered them.

The wolf, distant relative to the dogs we know today, was bolder than the fox, and sometimes preyed on the settlers' stray livestock. He was an excellent trap-robber too, and his heavy coat, powerful shoulders and legs, and very strong jaws enabled him to thrive in the cold northern winters.

The buffalo, or bison, has roamed the earth for thousands of years. Although he has changed some since our first knowledge of his existence, this rather awkward beast has always been a source of food and clothing to man. Early man, primitive in his abilities and lacking all but the crudest of weapons, depended heavily on this animal. Stone-tipped spears and clubs wielded by a number of men at once were probably required to fell a huge bison. When the hunting party returned with great chunks of meat and thick-furred hides there was rejoicing and a feast. Evidence of prehistoric man's dependency on animals for food and clothing can be seen in very old paintings and crude carvings discovered in various parts of the world. Some of the most famous prehistoric paintings are those on the walls of caves near Altamira, Spain. Several, including the one on page 31, depict the bison hunt. Like the others, it was painted with ground earth pigments mixed in natural oils, and painstakingly applied to the stone surface. Although the artist was a primitive, you can recognize the subject at once. Don't you agree that the artist exaggerated those features which most readily identify the animal—the sharp horns, massive hump, strong legs with sharp hooves? It's easy to look at the painting and know that this animal was dangerous to hunt. The sensitive attention to details of line and the rich color of the body tell us also that here was an animal revered by man, perhaps thought to be even beautiful. These paintings were probably made between 20,000 and 50,000 years ago, during what is sometimes called the Ice Age and sometimes the Old Stone Age.

The deer, a beautiful animal found in abundance in many parts of the United States, is sure-footed, quiet, and a very fast runner. His large ears and sensitive nose warn him of danger, and his lean, powerful legs carry him quickly away from it. The white-tail buck pictured on page 33 is not easily seen against the trees. His gray-brown coat blends with the autumn hues. Many a hunter has passed close to a deer without knowing it. The deer's smooth lines and handsome proportions are crowned by a magnificent head and rack of antlers. He is truly one of nature's beautiful creatures.

The goddess Bastet.

34

A Very Old Cat from Egypt

The cat on page 34 seems to have a waiting air. Perhaps she is still expecting to be returned to her home in Egypt where she was honored and well cared for some 2,000 years ago. This statue was created to personify the goddess Bastet, also called Bast. Although the Egyptians did not worship cats or other animals, sometimes they depicted their gods and goddesses in animal form. The sculptor managed to give this cat statuette an air of serenity and nobility which the Egyptians believed a goddess would have.

Note the ear rings adorning Bastet. You can also see traces of the necklace which they put around her neck. The surfaces of the statue are mottled and pitted now, but probably were once smooth and glossy.

Cats were held in respect by the Egyptians to such an extent that they mummified dead pets, and when a house cat died, members of the household would go into mourning for it. Egyptians felt that cats were of great service to them, as indeed they were. Stored cereal grains, the main food for the people, were often infested by hordes of mice and rats. Only the cats could save the grain from destruction, and for this protection the Egyptians were most grateful. The penalty for killing a cat was death.

If you are fond of cats, you may be interested in learning more about them and their different characteristics. You might consult an encyclopedia and books about cats for information about Persian and Angora cats—the long-haired beauties; Siamese cats, which are considered the aristocrats of the short hairs; the Manx cat, which is born with only a stub tail; and the tortoise-shell cat, which got its name because of its mottled coat.

You will find it interesting to collect pictures of cats—especially kittens.

Horses Come in Different Styles

It is just as much fun to study lines and proportions in horses as in cats and dogs, even more fun if you happen to like horses better. There is considerable variation of lines and contours in the horse (equine) family. Types range from race horses to Shetland ponies, and from zebras to army mules. The race horse in full action is a splendid example of concerted, rhythmic movement. It is worth a trip to the race track to see and hear these magnificent animals thunder past on their way to the finish line. Watch the rippling flow of the muscles as the legs come forward and then drive back.

The race horse on page 36 is Citation putting on a burst of speed as he comes down the home stretch to win. The artist, C. W. Anderson, knows horses very well. Dating from his early days on the plains of Nebraska, he has studied horses and their characteristics. In the following paragraph, he tells you in his own words why he chose to depict Citation this way.

"Citation in the Home Stretch."

I have always been a great admirer of Citation, considering him to be our greatest horse since Man O'War. He had unusual beauty and was perfection itself in action. His stride was so smooth and rhythmic that he seemed to flow over the ground. In this lithograph I chose that split second before he is off the ground with all four feet because the sweep of line of the near foreleg is carried through the shoulder and neck to the tip of the ears in a driving tangent that to me gives the feeling I had in watching him cut loose with the surging drive that smothered his opposition.

With his skillful drawing the artist has made us feel the power and drive of the running horse. The jockey, standing in his stirrups, crouches low over Citation's neck. He almost seems to be part of the horse. The feeling of speed is accentuated by the flying mane and tail, and by the clouds of dust where Citation's hooves have dug into the dirt track. Most important in creating the feeling of swift movement is the line mentioned by the artist in the paragraph above. The line of the right front leg, up over the neck to the tips of the ears, expresses the dynamic quality of the horse's action.

You will notice that the artist omitted any suggestion of the race track in the background. If he had added any items such as the bleachers filled with excited people, or even the rails alongside the track, they would have distracted attention from the horse.

Race horses of many kinds have been favorite subjects of artists. The drawing on this page shows us harness racers. These horses do not gallop, but run with heads held high, pulling along two-wheeled sulkies. The drawing illustrates these strong-muscled and swift pacers as they round a turn. The artist has eliminated unnecessary detail, relying on dark masses and quick strokes to catch the racers in action. The sketchy treatment of the horses' legs suggests rapid movement, as if the eye were unable to catch sight of them as they thunder by with pounding hooves.

Present-day sculptors have used the horse form to create many splendid effects. Instead of realistic forms, they sometimes make what might be called "design horses." The race horse on page 38 is certainly not a real looking animal and neither is the jockey realistic. This is a rather playful interpretation of a jockey on his thoroughbred as it prances to the starting post. Slender proportions are exaggerated,

some of the surfaces are flattened, and the whole effect is one of strength and lean grace. Such details as the jockey's face, and the stirrups, bridle, and reins have been omitted. This serves to center our attention upon the spirited horse, who is eager to be off.

The great horse in the picture on page 39 is in striking contrast to the prancing steed on page 38. His huge body is emphasized by curves which make you think of the power of his bulging muscles. You may have seen this type of horse at a county fair where Percherons and Belgians have been exhibited. They are called draft horses because they are bred to pull heavy loads. Draft horses have been almost entirely replaced in our country by trucks and heavy machinery, but when we see them in the show ring or as a matched six-horse team in a parade, the effect is one of powerful, dramatic beauty.

The war chargers ridden by knights in the Middle Ages were strong, heavy

"The Jockey," by Hunt Diedrich.

horses which could bear the weight of the steel armor worn by their riders. It is said that the knights sometimes wore armor so heavy that they could not climb onto their horses without assistance.

The jockey and his horse make us feel the excitement of the horse and his eagerness to break into action. But in the case of the war charger, there is little effect of movement. The charger stands with all four feet planted firmly on the ground and the rider sits easily in the saddle. The sword points downward while the rider, St. Martin, holds up his coat as though he were about to hand it to someone on the ground.

St. Martin lived in the fourth century, a very long time ago. One of the things for which he was remembered was the gift of his coat to a beggar. This is the incident in his life which the sculptor chose to portray.

St. Martin was born a heathen in Pannonia, an ancient country of central Europe. As a young soldier he was converted to Christianity and eventually became the bishop of Tours, France. He is famous for his stand against drunkenness and because he tried to prevent the slaughter of the Priscillianist heretics.

His coat became a venerated possession of the Frankish kings, who carried it about in a portable shrine. His feast, Martinmas, is November 11th. In England, the warm, balmy weather about

that time of the year, which corresponds to our Indian summer, is called St. Martin's summer.

After reading this story about St. Martin, look again at his picture. The statue should now have a new meaning to you, and you can see how the sculptor symbolized the life of St. Martin in a modern work of art.

Horses are a popular subject with painters as well as with sculptors. An American artist, Phil Paradise, painted the picture shown on page 40. He called it "Moonlight Madness." The horses are stirring about in the pasture back of the barn, excited and playful in the light of the moon. It seems as though

"St. Martin," by Sidney Waugh.

39

"Moonlight Madness."

the forms are really moving as you look at the picture. You can almost hear the hooves on the ground, and the whinnies of these animals as they nudge each other playfully. In this picture the moonlit horse forms are the center of interest. They are more important than the tree, barn, farmhouse, or sky. Everything is subordinated to the animal movement. Remember this, because later on you will learn more about this principle of art, which is called *emphasis.*

Art and Animals

It is a good idea to round up our ideas occasionally and find out what we have learned. Here are some points to remember from our study of beauty in animals.

1. Animals differ in proportion and shape, and some are more beautiful and interesting than others. It is fun to compare them. Discrimination will help us to see and enjoy beauty in the animal world.

40

2. "Good lines" are very important to beauty in animal forms just as they are in automobiles or airplanes.

3. Fine proportions are characteristic of beautifully built animals. Proportions that are not well balanced disturb our sense of beauty.

4. Contrasts of light and dark and color make some animals more interesting in appearance. Look again at the German shepherds on page 25, and the fox on page 27.

5. The texture of an animal's fur may contribute greatly to his beauty. For example, compare the fur of a fox with the hide of an elephant.

6. Movement is an important factor in the beauty of an animal. Some animals move with smooth, gliding action. Others simply waddle.

EXPERIENCES IN APPRECIATION

1. Select an animal family for study of lines and proportions. You might take the dog family, including the wolf, fox, and coyote, or the rodents, including the rabbit, squirrel, and woodchuck. Make a series of simple sketches showing characteristic lines in each member of the family.

2. Start a collection of animal pictures. Organize your selections to show animals which have particularly pleasing lines, proportions, and textures; those built for swift action and those revealing great strength.

3. Observe animals at the circus, in the zoo, and on the farm. Watch their movements. Write "word pictures" describing their characteristic movements.

4. Study the work of the great animal painter, Rosa Bonheur. Collect copies of her paintings and tell the class what you have learned about her work and her life.

5. Study the work of Frederic Remington, the American artist who painted the "Wild West." If possible, secure one of the books which he illustrated and show it to your classmates.

6. Arrange a day for an exhibition of small animal statues. Bring to class any small animal figures which you can secure. These may include wood carvings, pottery, soap carvings, or glass animals. Discuss these animal figures for the points listed above.

CREATIVE ACTIVITIES

1. Choose an animal family and make a series of sketches showing characteristics of different members of the family. Work from live animals when possible.

2. Choose one animal with which you are familiar. Make sketches of the animal in typical poses.

3. Choose an animal which you think has a decidedly individual, characteristic style of movement. Draw it in action. Is it smooth and fast, slow and easy, quick and jerky, or clumsy? Experiment with different kinds of lines to see which ones will best express the characteristic action.

4. Hold an exhibition of the animal drawings made by the class. Select a judge to choose the three which he likes best and to tell you his reasons.

5. When you study Chapter 8 on sculpture you will find more examples of animals as seen through the eyes of sculptors. Included are some fine examples of animal sculpture by pupils your age. You will learn about a variety of materials that can be used to help you create animal sculptures of your own.

Trees, Clouds, Wind and Water

Chapter Four

Some people think that trees have beauty only when they are in full leaf. Perhaps these people value trees only as shade from the sun. Other people know that trees may be very interesting, even beautiful, when bare of all leaves. Indeed, tree branches are sometimes even more beautiful when bare than when covered with foliage. Why? Because some bare tree branches make wonderful patterns against the sky. Of course, if you think of tree branches only as a support for leaves in the summertime you may not understand this; however, with a little study you will see the beauty in their lines as they reach out, whether they are lacy and fragile or thick and strong.

Patterns in Tree Branches

There are as many different patterns in tree branches as there are trees in the world. It is this endless variety which adds so much interest to the study of tree patterns. However, trees of the same species do show the same characteristic lines of growth in their branches. There are many beautiful types of tree branchings that you might see in your own backyard or along the street. These are common trees, the kind that grow in many parts of the country. Look first at the pattern of the locust, on page 44. You will see at once that it is different from many kinds of trees. It is irregular, with sudden little turns at unexpected places— a staccato movement. There is surprise in every branch.

The other trees on page 44 are the elm and the maple. At first glance, the line of growth may seem similar in the two trees. But then you see the branches of the maple in the first picture spread out fanlike and curve skyward. They form a symmetrical pattern, round and full like the top half of a circle. The lower branches grow straight out from

43

Locust trees in winter. An irregular pattern with staccato movement.

the trunk, which makes the maple an excellent shade tree. The branches of the elm also spread out like a fan, but they grow nearly straight up, then begin to curve gradually outward. Some of the heavy outer branches curve earthward in a graceful arc. The elm grows tall and stately, and lends dignity to fine homes and lawns.

Artists have discovered the beauty of trees in winter and are sometimes moved to paint the tracery of bare tree branches against the snow and sky. The painting called "No More Room at the Inn" by Lauren Ford, an American woman, is a charming scene, and a familiar one to people who live in the northeastern part of the United States. This picture is full of human interest. We like the children, the horses, the barns, and the old house. But think how

A maple tree with radiating branches, full and round.

An elm tree with fanlike spread, tall and stately.

A painting by Lauren Ford called "No More Room at the Inn."

"A Pear Tree," by Edward Bruce.

deserted the place would seem without the trees. They make a fascinating pattern against the snow and sky. Their curved branches in contrast to the straight lines of the buildings give added life to the painting.

Still another pattern is found in the fruit trees that bloom in the spring. The painting called "A Pear Tree" by Edward Bruce is a lovely interpretation of delicate, white pear blossoms against a blue sky.

A Closeup Look

How often have you stopped to look at a tree closely? The bark of a tree is beautiful, too, and very interesting. A look at the closeup photographs on page 47 will show you how trees differ in bark patterns.

The bark of ponderosa pine, the first photo, is furrowed, giving the appearance of great strength and old age. These trees grow very tall, and are straight and strong. As they grow the bark splits open, renewing itself from inside. The top surface is rough and scaly; flakes come off as the spring growth begins and the tree swells in size. This scaly surface makes a beautiful pattern of delicately shaded patches bordered by strong, deep, vertical furrows.

Compare such rugged texture with the smoother quaking-aspen bark. Here the bark hugs the tree closely, like a thin, tight skin, and has no rough scales or grooves. A series of irregularly spaced horizontal lines or wrinkles in

the bark climbs ladder-like up the tree to be lost in the foliage. This bark differs from that of the pine in another way. It grows with the tree instead of cracking open as the tree grows. It shows the stretch of growth in the wrinkles formed around the branch stubs. Only at the base where the bark is very thick does it show any splitting. Can you name another tree that has a horizontal growth pattern in its bark? How about the cherry tree? Or the birch?

The third example, the hemlock, has a rough bark somewhat similar to the pine, but the scales are smaller and more evenly spaced. Although at first glance the hemlock appears less rugged than the pine, actually it is rougher. This tree has what is called a shaggy bark. The sections or scales turn out at the sides and bottom, giving them the appearance of very old shingles. And their purpose is the same as shingles, to protect the tree as shingles protect a house.

Try some "closeups" yourself. Compare the textures of the bark from several trees. Can you find interesting patterns such as shown on page 47? How do old trees differ from young ones? What trees in your neighborhood have the most interesting bark?

Trees in Summertime

Nearly everyone enjoys the sight of a fine tree in full leaf on a summer day. Such a tree may appeal to some people chiefly because it provides shade; if it

BARK TEXTURES

A. *Ponderosa pine (right). Rugged and furrowed, showing great strength.*

B. *Quaking aspen (left, below). A thin, tight skin-like bark with horizontal growth pattern.*

C. *Hemlock (right, below). A shaggy bark, with "shingles" to protect the tree.*

U. S. FOREST SERVICE

7

48

is a fruit tree some will think first of its delicious fruit; if it is a very large tree some will think of its beautiful wood. However, people who have learned to get the most enjoyment from trees will look at a splendid tree also for its beauty. They will note its shape. Is it tall and stately? Or low and spreading? Are the masses of foliage interesting in shape?

No matter in what part of the country you may live, you will find trees that are beautiful. The three trees on page 48 grow in widely separated sections of the country. The great elm tree stands in Durham, New Hampshire. Perhaps you have passed it on a vacation trip. It is a magnificent sight with its great masses of foliage that sway gracefully in the breeze. There are many of these giant elms in New England and other eastern states; everyone should learn to know them. The second tree, a eucalyptus, is in Fresno County, California. It is as graceful as the elm tree, but in its own characteristic way. Notice the great masses of delicate, lacy foliage. If you live in California you surely know these large trees with their waxy, dark leaves. If you plan to visit the state, remember to look for the beautiful eucalyptus trees.

The enormous oak tree pictured on page 48 stands in the city of Austin, Texas. Estimated to be over 500 years old, it is known as Treaty Oak because it is believed that many years ago a boundary-line treaty with the Indians was made here. In those days the branches could not have been so low. Its lower branches actually rest upon the ground. The whole effect is that of great strength and age.

The three pictures you have just studied will help acquaint you with trees in full leaf and also with tree shapes. The white elm is a graceful tree which has been compared to a vase of flowers. The eucalyptus grows differently, its masses of foliage creating a tall, domelike shape. The old oak has grown into a broad, spreading mass. How many trees that grow in your locality can you recognize by their characteristic shapes?

The search for beauty in trees with bare branches or in full foliage is a fascinating hobby. There is beauty, too, in forests or groves where trees grow close together. The forest scene on page 50 has a stirring, wonderful beauty. Great tree trunks reaching to the skies create a strong pattern of vertical lines, and the sunlight filtering through from above makes a delightful play of light and shadow. Notice the interesting texture of the bark on the tree trunks in the foreground.

Quite a change from the straight sentinels of the forest are the trees on page 51. Unique to the South, these are live oaks in Louisiana. In that warm, moist climate, vegetation thrives better than in dry areas. One can find things growing there that won't grow in the North, or in the hot deserts. This is evidenced by the moss hanging from the branches of the oaks. Looking up

50

through these trees, one feels he might be in an enchanted forest. How beautiful this grove must be when the wind breathes through the moss, causing it to sway gently, creating moving, lacelike patterns. The branches of the trees seem to be spreading gracefully to display the moss growing upon them. Like all oaks, the branches twist and turn in sturdy curves, as if they were sure of each movement. It is this growth pattern that gives oaks the appearance of

great strength. Like the Treaty Oak, these trees are very old, for their branches spread far out and almost touch the ground in places. Anyone visiting Louisiana or other Gulf coast states may see trees draped with this beautiful lacy moss.

Probably one of the most interesting trees of all is the banyan. Its strange-sounding name seems appropriate, doesn't it? Look at the picture at the top of page 52. Notice how the

Live oaks in Louisiana, showing the lacy pattern of moss growing from the branches.

U. S. FOREST SERVICE

Banyan Tree. Growing extra legs for support, these trees grow out and down as well as up.

branches grow out from the trunk, then reach down to the ground to support themselves as they wander off. They appear to be standing on many legs. They make an interesting pattern of vertical lines and near-vertical angles. Of course, these trees can best be appreciated in color. Their rich, sunwarmed tans and grays make them stand out in subtle contrast to the greens in the leaves and other vegetation. The sunlight filtering through from above adds a warm glow, producing a dappled pattern on trunks and the ground below. This giant banyan tree, growing on the grounds of the Ringling Museum of Art in Sarasota, Florida, is typical of the exotic tree forms to be found in this state.

Trees are nearly always more beautiful when we view them as part of a larger natural scene. At the beginning of the chapter we discussed several tree forms that we might find growing near our homes or some other place close by. The winter branches we saw seemed a bit out of place, because we saw them alone. On page 54 are two photo-

52

graphs in color of trees and landscapes. The photos show the contrast between trees in autumn and winter. The delicate, dark branches of the trees in the upper photograph are especially beautiful against the sky and reflected in the water below. Don't you agree that the word "serenity" describes this scene well? The stillness of the water and the soft blue over the entire scene are quiet as a whisper. Yet this photo has both contrast and variety, created by the thin, dark lines of the branches and the larger masses of snow next to still water. Have you ever had an opportunity to see a beautiful winter landscape such as this?

The lower photograph displays the beauty of trees in early autumn, with their brilliant and many-colored patterns. The contrasting dark green foliage and emerald grass create a handsome setting for the farm buildings. Farmers take advantage of trees in many ways. Trees provide effective windbreaks against winter's cold, and hold back the drifting snow. Trees near the house keep it cooler on hot days by providing shade.

State governments maintain forestry departments to protect their trees; they realize that thoughtless or greedy people might one day destroy the remaining forest lands of our country.

Artists have studied the beauty of form and pattern in trees since landscape painting was first attempted. An American painter named Daniel Garber is well known as a painter of trees.

The magnificent old tree on page 55 is a fine example of his paintings. Study the strong, graceful curves in the sturdy branches, the billowy masses of foliage, and the interesting play of light and shadow in the leaves and on the trunk. Notice especially the great branch hanging almost to the ground. See how the weight of this mass is balanced on the other side by the long branch that swings upward and to the left.

The photograph on page 56 was taken early in the morning. The sun is low in the sky, so it throws long shadows on the ground. It isn't often we see scenes like this. The sun is at the level of the trees and shines through them, creating an almost luminous effect in the background. This effect is called *backlighting*. It's used by artists and photographers alike to produce unusual lights and shadows in their compositions.

Trees in the Wind

Trees are fascinating subjects for lovers of beauty to study at any season of the year. In winter there are the intricate patterns of bare branches, in spring the lacy new growth of budding leaves, in summer the glory of full foliage, and in autumn the spectacle of gorgeous color. Sometimes it is the wind that turns designer, and gives our trees new forms. When tall and slender young trees sway with the breeze, there is rhythm in the way they all move at once. When a stiffer breeze blows, the

WESTERN PENNSYLVANIA CONSERVANCY

W. GEORGE THORNTON

54

A painting by Daniel Garber called "Old Tree, Chalfont."

trees bend, forming more forceful line patterns. Can you recall a time during a storm when the trees seemed to be straining together against the force of the wind?

"Winter Sun," by Wendell Orosz

The picture on page 57 was painted by Wendell Orosz, a young American artist who had no formal art training. His natural talent and feeling for art expression brought him success.

"Winter Sun" is the kind of painting which helps us to see new kinds of beauty in nature—beauty that we would have missed if we had not seen the painting. Our attention is caught by the pattern of the bare trees seen against the houses and hills. The large branches swinging to the left help to create a fascinating design. Notice how the shadows of the branches on the snow echo the movement toward the left. It seems as though the winds of winter must have swept the branches along their way, but we also feel the dynamic quality in the lines of growth as tree trunks and branches have thrust up.

Probably you will never see an

55

Backlighting produces striking pattern of light and shadow.

56

actual scene like that in "Winter Sun," but you might see nature the way that Wendell Orosz would see it. The artist does not put all the details of nature into his picture. Instead he selects the features which are important in creating a beautiful effect. Perhaps you can think of details which the painter of "Winter Sun" omitted in order to create the effect that he desired.

Beautiful Effects in Water

Since oceans, lakes, rivers, and brooks take up so much space in our world, it is fortunate that in them we find innumerable glimpses of beauty. These beautiful effects found in water vary greatly. The surface of a lake may act as a mirror. This happens only when the water is still and no wind ruffles its surface. When water tumbles over a waterfall and swirls away, the effect is very different. The first photograph on page 59 is a good example of turbulent water. Frothy white lines with constantly changing patterns can hold our attention for long periods. Such a sight can be awe-inspiring, especially when we stand near a waterfall or rapids where great quantities of water move quickly through a gorge.

A more gentle surface effect created by moving water is that shown in the bottom picture. The regular ripples in

"Winter Sun," by Wendell Orosz.

JAMES WESTOVER

the surface make a quietly moving pattern. This is a familiar sight to people who have watched the movement of a calm sea or the rippled surface of a lake.

When there is little or no wind to disturb the water's surface, reflections play an important part in producing beautiful effects. In the center picture the water is mirror-smooth. The result is a reflection of the snow-covered trees above, truly a scene to delight the eye. Have you ever had an opportunity to watch the sharp, clear reflections on water this smooth?

Some effects on the water's surface come and go so quickly that the eye must be alert to catch their beauty. The camera's eye caught the fine effect shown on page 60. The canoe paddle produced the pattern of circles as it was lifted from the water. Notice how the reflection of the paddle adds interest to the composition.

Relate to the class a description of some beautiful water effect you have seen. Did the effect depend on line patterns in ripples or waves, effect of light and dark, or reflections for its beauty?

The ocean gives us certain effects that are not possible in smaller lakes or rivers. When the great ocean waves come rolling in and break against the rocky shore the effect is splendidly dramatic. The seascape on page 60, called "Meridian," was painted by Frederick J. Waugh, a famous American artist. He has made his picture interesting through the sharp contrasts of white water and dark rocks and through the effects of sunlight and shadow. Here we can feel the tremendous power of the sea as the great waves thunder in and crash against the rocks. This kind of painting is very realistic. The artist shows us the sea as it actually looks.

In Mr. Waugh's painting we felt the excitement and strength of the sea. On page 61 is a lithograph by Joe Jones, who sees the water in a very different way. We can be sure he found contentment in this scene, for with a sure, yet delicate, line he has captured a peaceful mood. He must have chosen a clearing sky for a special reason. Don't you think he felt the freshness in the air just as you do after a storm? The men in the boat close to us in the picture seem to be preparing to hoist their sail. One feels that they'll get the sail up just as the clouds pass over. The day will be bright, and the breeze fresh and clean.

Clouds Tell a Story

Clouds tell the story of the weather. When we look at the sky and see huge masses of dense clouds above us, we say, "It's going to rain." And near the end of the storm, when we see the blue of the sky showing through, we say, "The storm is over!" What shapes of clouds do you see when you think of an approaching storm? Have you ever looked into the sky on a hot summer day, to see only a few white puffs that seem to hang there motionless? Do you

WESTERN PENNSYLVANIA CONSERVANCY

PHOTO BY MIKE AND LYNN SIMS

WESTERN PENNSYLVANIA CONSERVANCY

"Water Rings," a photograph by Ernest Schnizer.

"Meridian," a painting by Frederick Waugh.

"Reaching for the Sun," a lithograph by Joe Jones.

recall having looked up to see those wispy, silken threads stretched out for great distances high up in the sky? Clouds like these often tell us of a change in the weather that may be a day or two away.

Some people enjoy looking at clouds to find the shapes of things they know. Other folks just like to look at clouds because it makes them "feel good." Haven't you felt a thrill in watching great cloud forms glide silently across the sky? And surely the softly tinted shapes in a fading sunset give you a feeling of contentment and joy at just

being alive as they lie there unmoving on the horizon, their arms stretching high to catch the last warm light of the setting sun.

The illustration on page 62 shows how clouds can help to make a good picture. Without clouds this picture wouldn't be nearly so interesting nor would it give you a feeling of great distance as it does now. Reflections in the gently rippling waters increase the beauty which the setting sun imparts to the clouds. The boats and shorelines also play an important role. They contrast sharply with the soft cloud masses

61

and water to create interesting dark
patterns. Look for pictures like this
yourself. Don't forget your camera!

Sometimes we overlook beauty in
the "ordinary" things because we see
them so often that we become used to
them. An American artist named John
Rogers Cox shows us that a scene which
might look ordinary at first glance can
be both beautiful and unusual. In this
painting, "Wheat Shocks," Mr. Cox
tells us a story about a farmer. One can
almost believe he is standing with us,
looking past the rotted old fence post
toward his field of drying wheat. The

cloud standing motionless in the deep
blue sky emphasizes the loneliness of
the scene. Do you, too, feel the heat
rising from the dry earth as the wheat
shocks stretch in lonely vigil as far as
the eye can see? How glad the farmer
must be that his summer's work has
been so successful.

In the Japanese print shown on page
64, the artist has combined the elements mentioned in the title of this
chapter—trees, clouds, wind, and
water. In this case the rain falls from
the dark clouds and is driven across
our vision at an angle by a strong wind.

Tree branches in the foreground bend and sway in the wind. Farther away, growing dimmer in the distance, other tree branches bow their heads under the force of the wind and rain. Two pedestrians going down the hill protect themselves from the rain, one with an umbrella and the other with his big hat. Still others climb the hill at a slower pace. The first one is shielded from the rain by his big hat and straw raincoat. The other two are coolies, carrying a litter. A passenger on the litter is almost entirely covered with some kind of tarpaulin.

In this print the artist had no thought of realism, but rather was trying to create a decorative effect. There is a rhythmic pattern with delicate graduations of light and dark. This rhythm is created by parallel lines suggesting the rain, by the repeated pattern of the branches in lighter shades, and the line of the hill. These are combined to produce a pleasant pattern that is decorative and tells a story at the same time. Japanese prints, perhaps more than any others, show this attention to beauty of form and line, to harmony of movement which we have called rhythm.

Have you ever noticed the special kind of beauty that hovers over the landscape on a rainy day? Trees, hills,

"Wheat Shocks," a painting by John Rogers Cox.

63

Leon Falk, Jr.

and buildings seem to be painted in delicate tones of silver grays. Ugliness is blotted out by a strange, mysterious beauty. On the next rainy day, look carefully, and perhaps you will see a magic transformation of some familiar scene.

Beauty Is Where You Find It

In our study of art so far we have found beauty both in nature and in things made by man. Animals and airplanes, trees and automobiles, often provide us with moments of special enjoyment, particularly if we can recognize those elements which combine to produce the most pleasing results— good proportions, balance, emphasis, and other art principles. While we can recognize beautiful things without knowing the "why" of it, to know these principles and how they are used both in nature and in man-made products can help us to enjoy beauty wherever we find it.

EXPERIENCES IN APPRECIATION

1. Collect pictures of trees which you think are beautiful. Explain the chief claim to beauty for each tree.

2. Collect pictures of oceans, lakes, and streams. Try particularly to get different effects. Use pictures that include interesting or dramatic cloud formations. Label each picture to explain why the effect is beautiful.

3. Write a description of some effect in water that you have seen and thought

beautiful. Trying to match words to what we see with our eyes often helps to increase our enjoyment of beauty.

4. If you have a camera try to get a good picture of the most beautiful tree you can find. If several members of the class can do this, plan a day for an exhibition of tree snapshots by class members. Perhaps you will enjoy making a hobby of tree pictures. Try to get the same tree in all four seasons of the year and also when the wind is blowing.

CREATIVE ACTIVITIES

1. Make a series of "tree portraits." Select three trees of distinctly different types. Make a pencil drawing showing characteristic growth and formation. Make a series of color sketches of trees, using water color, crayons, or soft chalk.

2. If you should make a hobby of tree pictures, you will find it interesting to make portraits of the same trees in different seasons and during different kinds of weather. The same tree in winter on a fine, sunny day, or during a snowstorm gives very different effects. On a windy day in spring or on a rainy day in November it will show still different effects. Probably there will not be time for you to carry out all these projects as classwork, but they are good suggestions for fun outside of school if you like to draw and paint.

3. Plan a dramatic, story-telling picture of trees. The success of your picture will depend on how well you imagine the effect that you wish to create. You might wish to produce an effect that is strange, weird, and frightening. Or you might prefer to make a picture which expresses gaiety and lively happiness. There are many other effects which you might choose. The first thing to do is to decide upon the effect which you intend to create. Next, experiment with various ways of producing it. As you can see, this picture will require both thought and imagination on your part.

What kind of story does this tree tell? How would you complete the picture?

Our World of Color

The study of color is a fascinating science. To understand this science you need to know something about the characteristics of light, for it is light that produces color.

Light is a form of radiant energy. Because of this energy, light travels by means of waves. You know that the brightest source of light is the sun. Light from the sun produces the variety of colors visible to the human eye.

What Is Color?

Light from the sun, or from a spotlight, or from the lamp in your living room, is made up of many colors. You can see these colors separately by placing a prism in a bright beam of sunlight. The light that comes through the prism will be separated into bands of color from red through violet. When you see a rainbow you are witnessing the same thing. The raindrops act like small prisms, breaking the white light into its color components. These colors are called the *visible spectrum*.

When you see a particular color, such as red or green, you are seeing light waves reflected from a surface. As stated above, white light contains all colors when it reaches an object. Why then do we see only certain colors reflected back to our eyes? This is because the chemical construction of materials varies—one material may absorb all but the red light waves, another all but green, and so on.

Color scientists have discovered many chemicals and materials that change the way surfaces reflect color. These are made into dyes for cloth, paints, cosmetics, plastics, and many other items.

The Painter and His Colors

For many centuries, artists made their own colors, using natural pigments and oil. Early cave dwellers used earth colors or pigments and animal oils to make paints. They probably applied them to the cave walls with their fingers, pieces of hide, or wood strips. See page 31. Many famous artists of the past made colors by grinding clays, minerals, vegetable roots, and even certain insects. It is possible today to buy artists' colors, house paints, lacquers, plastic sprays, and even metallic paints at a hardware store.

Color Has Multiple Uses

Painters are not the only artists who use color. Colors are used by home decorators, who plan color schemes to suit a family; they are used by industrial engineers, who devise color safety systems to prevent accidents; they are used by industrial designers to make a product beautiful; they are used by advertisers, who design posters, magazine advertisements, and packages to sell a product; and they are used by housewives in making clothing, decorating their homes, and making meals more attractive.

How Colors Affect Us

Scientific tests have revealed a great deal of surprising information about color. Warm colors are exciting, and can actually increase your blood pressure. Cool colors are quieting, and cause reductions in blood pressure. Splashes of bright color are very stimulating, but it isn't good to look at them too long. They can make you feel tired after a while. Large areas of grayed, cold tones are depressing.

Colors influence our emotions. Circus wagons and children's toys are usually painted in light, bright reds and yellows because these colors create a feeling of excitement and happiness. Rich bright blues and purples are exciting too, but less so than reds and yellows. Light warm tones like peach, yellow, and light orange make us feel sociable, while light cool tones of green and blue make us calm and at ease.

There is scientific evidence to show that colors have significant effects on a person's performance. This is true whether he is working at a machine, doing homework, or eating dinner. Schools, office buildings, libraries, and hospitals are often color-planned. Modern schoolrooms painted in brighter tones reflect more light and keep students alert and happy. Library study rooms painted in cool tones relieve eye strain and have a quieting effect. Hospital rooms are painted in both warm and cool colors. Can you explain why?

Yellow is the easiest color to see. It is used for caution signals, highway lane markers, and to indicate hazards such as steps that are hard to see. Black and yellow stripes are frequently used for marking dangerous obstructions.

When color is used to influence a person's efficiency, to warn of danger, or for that matter, to change a person's state of mind in any way, it is called *functional color.*

Color Makes the Meaning Clear

We have learned through experience to associate colors with certain words or phrases. You can demonstrate this to yourself by choosing colors which you think best suit a word or phrase. Read the words below, then think of the color or combination of colors you would use with the word. After you have done all eight, compare your selections with those on the opposite page. Do you agree?

1. Danger!
2. Happiness
3. Loneliness
4. Sadness
5. Excitement!
6. Warmth
7. Cold
8. Silence

This short test of your feeling for color was designed to demonstrate how colors are used to make a meaning clear. Imagine a painting of a circus, but without color—only black and white and gray. Would it be very likely to capture the real spirit and meaning of a circus? Color brings a painting to life. It appeals to us through our emotions. We often enjoy a colorful picture more because we understand it better.

Success Stories—In Color

The success of an artist largely depends on how he tells his story. For centuries painters have sensed the role of color in making clear the meanings of their paintings. The master painters of earlier times had no scientific evidence to help them select colors. Their choices depended partly upon how they felt about a subject. But their successes with color were by no means accidental. None of us needs scientific evidence to explain how color in a painting affects us. We can feel it. And the color may match any of our moods, emotions, or mental states, including confusion!

In Chapter 9, Fine Paintings to Remember, you'll study the major painting styles of the last hundred years or so—from about 1850 to the present day. Each of the next four paragraphs refers to a painting done in a different style. Notice the meaningful ways in which the painters used their colors.

What does the word "romantic" mean to you? Its true meaning has to do with adventure. Romantic painters portrayed the hunt, feats of bold men, and semi-mythical tales. These were exciting paintings, full of action. Turn to page 179 and look at "The Lion Hunt." Splashes of rich warm colors against dark blues and greens suggest both excitement and mystery. The deep, elegant colors of the men's clothing indicate that this was a sport reserved especially for wealthy men. From what you have learned about color, tell in your own words why the artist selected the colors he did. Remember how warm colors affect us. Which colors suggest strange things and unknown dangers?

COLOR MAKES THE MEANING CLEAR

Here are eight word-color matches. You may have chosen different colors, and this is good!—as long as they match the word. Read the comments with each color block below.

DANGER! — *a color that says "Stop!—Stay away."*

EXCITEMENT! — *light and bright, alive!*

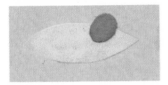

HAPPINESS — *light colors, warm and bright.*

WARMTH — *colors in the red end of the spectrum.*

LONELINESS — *a depressing state of mind, dull colors.*

COLD — *colors in the blue end of the spectrum. Which is the coldest color?*

SADNESS — *a deep personal hurt, dark colors without vitality.*

SILENCE — *nothingness, a dark place without life.*

A group of painters in Paris grew tired of painting things in a realistic way. They developed a style that fairly shouted for attention. Because their work was so bold and different, these painters were known as "Les Fauves," which means the wild beasts. Turn to page 182 and look at "The Red Studio." Would you agree that the artist intended to shock people? If so, he certainly succeeded with his bold red painting. How does this color describe the feelings of the painter? The story is a very simple one—and it is clearly told.

Bright colors are exciting. So are strong contrasts. Look at the painting on page 185. The artist who painted this abstract design did not intend to tell a story with a definite meaning. Still, the effect is exciting, and color helps to make it so. The painting is titled simply "Improvisation No. 30." But it might be called "Attack," or "Sounds of a City." Both titles suggest action. Describe how you feel when you look at this painting.

Which colors would you select to paint a mysterious picture? See if your choice matches the painting on page 186. People usually associate mystery or the unknown with the night. Deep blues, purples, and blacks provide all sorts of hiding places for ghosts and night-people. This style of painting is Surrealism, the painting of dream worlds. What would happen to this painting if it were made in bright tones of yellow and orange?

A Lonely House

Now test yourself. On page 193 is a painting of a house. It was made by a high school student who was obviously moved by what he saw. Describe how the colors in this painting help make the meaning clear. After you have analyzed it yourself, read the comments about the picture on page 192.

Color and Competition

Color is an everyday affair. No matter where you may be at this moment there are colors in sight—in your school books, pencils, the walls and floor, your desk, and the clothing you are wearing. Most of the magazines you subscribe to and many advertisements are printed in color.

Advertising artists depend upon color to catch your eye and make their work appealing, so that you'll read it. They make it their business to know what colors can do. A billboard that advertises automobiles may be bright and rich in color. The observer is expected to feel excited about the prospect of owning that particular car. Have you noticed that sport models are usually pictured in red? Explain why. On the other hand, an artist may wish to emphasize the elegance of a particular model. In this case he'll use rich, dark colors, and allow the chrome to sparkle. A model, dressed in evening gown and furs, leans against the car, telling the prospect that this is truly an elegant automobile.

Sometimes color can be overworked in advertising. Full pages of products in color may not be as effective as a few color accents. Successful advertisers know that people won't read advertisements that are jumbled and confused. An easy-to-read, orderly arrangement has a much better chance of influencing the public than does a conglomeration of pictures and words.

Colors react to each other. An advertising artist knows how to take advantage of this fact to attract your attention. The next time you're in a supermarket, stroll down an aisle and take note of packages that stand out from the others. A few will shout for attention! The ones you'll notice will be brighter in color or will have more contrast. Black on white makes a strong contrast, and so does a bright color on a dull one. The greatest contrasts are between opposite colors (see page 76) of near-equal brightness. Test your eye on the first color sample below.

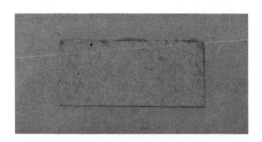

Your eyes cannot properly adjust to these two colors at the same time. To many viewers these colors will seem to shimmer as if they were lighted from behind. Look at the other two rectangles. The same shade of blue is used, but the background color has been changed to make it easier to look at. Which of the three would you use on a package? On a poster? Why?

Color in Your Home

Designers go to great lengths to create beautiful products for the home. Ranges, refrigerators, dishes, rugs, and hundreds of other things can be purchased in an amazing variety of colors. It would be a simple matter to fill the pages of this book with pictures of beautiful accessories and furniture. However, our concern is only to open your eyes to the possibilities for making your home more beautiful with color.

All of us have color preferences. The colors we like are the colors that make us feel good. Fortunately we can select or reject things to suit ourselves. That's the reason why furniture manufacturers make available hundreds of choices for fabric colors, patterns, and textures. And paint makers can match any one of a thousand shades, or create one to suit us exactly.

The colors we use in our homes should make us feel at home, whether they are bright, lively tones or cool, relaxing ones. Even though we have favorite colors, we probably wouldn't use the same ones in every room. Living rooms, kitchens, and bedrooms call for different colors, each to suit the family, but also the function of the room.

Two Rooms In Color

On page 226 is a friendly living room, decorated in rich, warm colors. These colors were selected by people who enjoy company. They entertain friends in this living room quite often —playing cards, discussing their pewter collection, or just chatting. Do you think the colors they selected are "right" for them? Would you feel welcome in this living room? How do you suppose the rest of the house is decorated?

A kitchen is a busy place. It's a workroom for your mother, a meeting place for friends, and sometimes a dining room too. It should be a cheerful place, with colors that are light and bright. Some kitchens are painted in tones of yellow and red. These colors suggest lots of activity and fun, but if they're too bright they may be hard on the eyes over long periods of time. Look at the kitchen on page 238. The colors here are crisp and clean, and reflect lots of light. Bright colors are used sparingly —just enough to make the room sparkle. Which other colors would be suitable for a kitchen? Read the comments about this kitchen on page 237. Would this kitchen suit you?

The Extra Things

Rooms are often designed with soft tones on the walls and basic furniture. The extra things add bright spots of color. The illustration opposite includes some articles that would brighten a home. When you look at this picture, be sure to study how the colors are used together. Each table is a separate color group, from the rich dark shades of the first table to the light, crisp tones of the last. Had you thought of fruits and vegetables as decorative items? Which table group is your favorite? Ours is the one at the right, near the top of the picture—the one with the carrots. Your selection might be the same, or any of the others. Tell which one you prefer, and why. Our selection was chosen because its color plan is ideal for a kitchen. Some of the others have colors that might be better suited to a living room, dining room, or bedroom. Choose the combination you would use in a living room. Tell why you made the choice.

The photograph of the gentleman looking over the collection of rugs on

Buffet Group, Designed by Don Wallance for
The Forecast Collection of Aluminum Company of America

*These aluminum housewares were designed with thought for both beauty and
functional quality.*

page 75 serves us in two ways. It displays some attractive and unusual rug designs and demonstrates how effective a color advertisement can be. The rugs in this illustration belong in a contemporary home. They would serve as accents in a room, probably repeating some colors already there. Take note of the restraint used in the selection of colors. Bright areas are small, so the rugs would not shout for attention. The three rugs with white backgrounds are fresh and clean in design. Try any of the three in the living room on page 227. Which colors do the rugs repeat? Where would you place one of these in the room?

In the next chapter you'll read more about this rug advertisement.

Color Mechanics

Color mechanics means the mixing of colors. Learning how to blend colors will not only add to your enjoyment of them but will also help you find shortcuts to colors when you need them. To make things interesting, you'll have a chance to experiment while you learn.

Spectrum Colors

The colors that come from white light are the spectrum colors. They are red, orange, yellow, green, blue, and violet. These are the six basic colors. By mixing each of these with its neighbor you produce the in-between colors of red-orange, yellow-orange, yellow-green, blue-green, blue-violet, and red-violet. The twelve colors you now have provide a good range to work with. These are the colors usually shown on a color circle.

The color circle on page 76 includes the spectrum colors and the six in between. These colors are spectrum bright, or full of strength. You seldom see them used at full strength on large areas. They're too bright to live with comfortably. They must be toned down first. You'll learn how to do this, and some other things besides.

The Properties of Color— Hue, Value, Intensity

As you learn more about using colors, you'll begin to think in terms of hue, value, and intensity. These are the properties of color. You are probably more or less familiar with these terms, but you might want to know exactly what they mean when used to describe color.

HUE is the property of a color that gives it its name—as red, yellow, blue.

VALUE is the property of a color that gives it lightness or darkness.

INTENSITY is the property of a color that gives it brightness.

Every color has a range of values from light to dark and a range of intensities from bright to dull. These ranges, or scales, are demonstrated on page 77, using the colors orange and blue. The horizontal bar is the intensity scale. The vertical bars are the value scales. The intensity scale is orange at one end, blue at the other. These are complementary colors, or directly op-

THE "COLLECTOR'S GROUP" OF CABIN CRAFTS RUGS.
COURTESY, CABIN CRAFTS, INC.

This handsome color advertisement suggests good-humored refinement and taste.
Carefully harmonized colors lend an air of elegance. Obviously the gentleman in
the picture is used to having only the best. Doesn't his attitude suggest that this
group of rugs is out of the ordinary?

75

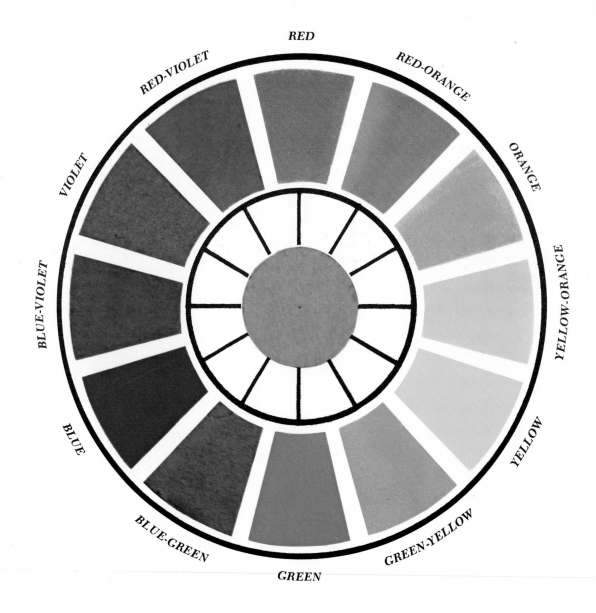

THE COLOR CIRCLE

Opposite colors are complements. When mixed they produce neutrals, as shown in the center.

SPECTRUM
/ORANGE

SPECTRUM
BLUE

VALUE SCALE

VALUE SCALE

INTENSITY SCALE

SCALES OF VALUE AND INTENSITY

*Intensity is strength or brightness. Value is lightness or darkness. The horizontal
bar is the intensity scale. The vertical bars are value scales.*

77

posite each other on the color circle. The tones in between are made by adding increasing amounts of the other color (the complement) until a neutral, or gray, is produced. The neutral is near the center of the bar. The value scale in the center is graduated from white to black.

A scale of intensities could be made for any color, light or dark. Every color also has a value scale, ranging from light to dark. The intensity does not change, but the value does. On the left side of page 77 you see a value scale for full intensity orange. The same kind of scale could be made for any of the other tones. Thousands of variations of any color are possible, but only a few are shown to demonstrate the method.

Try to recognize and understand the differences in hue, value, and intensity as you observe the world around you. There's no need for you to learn how to make these colors in order to use and enjoy them in your everyday life. But you'll have more fun with color if you learn to recognize those variations which are important in achieving fine color harmonies.

If you like to paint, here are some suggestions for experimenting with water colors. They'll help you to see the different effects which can be produced by using varying hues, values, and intensities. You may experiment at home on your own, or learn more about colors by working with them in your classroom.

Experiment to see what colors you can produce. Combine several pairs of complementary colors, adding small amounts of one color to the other. Use black too, if you wish. Adding water is a good way to make a color lighter, but the effect is different from that produced by adding white, as oil painters must do. It's not worthwhile to spend time making a color circle. Just experiment with the paints until you get the feel of it.

Understanding Color Harmonies

Our world of color is full of harmonies, colors that look as if they belong together. You'll find them in flowers, trees, window draperies, paintings, magazines, and numberless other examples. You'll also find disharmonious effects almost everywhere!

Your study of color harmony includes two main problems: (1) how to recognize good color harmony when you see it, and (2) how to create color harmony yourself. There are no exact rules to follow, but your knowledge of color properties will help. There are many occasions in everyday life when you'll want to combine colors so they will look right. Painting a room, planning a new spring outfit, and selecting colors for one of your own paintings are only a few of the ways in which you'll combine colors.

You made a start in learning about color harmony while considering the picture on page 73. There the colors seem to belong together—they show off each other's beauty, as in the case of the brilliant dishes on the blue cloth. A good general rule for selecting harmonious colors is to try them out on the eye. If the colors look as if they belong together, go ahead and use them.

> Plan a class session for experiments in combining colors harmoniously. Assemble a selection of colors from home—papers, cloths, and other items. A package of colored paper from the art supply shelf will help, too. Try combinations of two and three colors, then more. Remember to try it on the eye.

Monochromatic Harmony

The simplest type of color harmony is the monochromatic harmony, which consists of varying values and intensities of one hue. For example, a printed fabric might have a tan background with a pattern in tones of orange and brown. These colors all belong to the orange family, so they are not likely to disagree. See page 81.

Any one of the twelve colors on the color circle can be used for a monochromatic harmony, and any neutral— black, white, or gray—may be used with it. Neutrals have no color, so they can be used without changing the harmony.

Monochromatic color schemes are often used in dress. A girl might plan an outfit using different shades of blue, along with white for accent. See page 81. A boy may choose a brown suit, dark brown shoes, tan socks and tie, and a white shirt.

You'll observe many examples of monochromatic harmony in nature. The blue jay is one example, with blue feathers accented by black and white markings. The flamingo on page 84 is another, with soft tones of pink and white.

Report on examples of monochromatic harmony which you have seen in nature, pictures, or elsewhere.

Adjacents or Neighbor Colors— Good Harmonies

The colors which lie next to each other on the color circle are called adjacents. Two or more of these colors may be used to create an adjacent harmony. The coloring of leaves in the fall often contains adjacent harmonies. You'll see reds and yellows and, when the leaves are just beginning to turn, green, yellow-green, and yellow. See page 81.

You may enjoy experimenting with two or three adjacent colors. Some of the best color schemes are made from tints of neighboring colors.

Complementary Colors Can Be Harmonized

Color complements are always directly opposite each other on the color circle. There are six pairs of complements in the circle on page 76. These colors have a much more difficult time getting along together than adjacent colors. They are strangers, and when used together can produce very disagreeable effects. But reds and greens of different values and intensities can be used together, and the effect is surprisingly harmonious. A good red and

EASTMAN KODAK

COLOR SCHEMES OR HARMONIES

MONOCHROMATIC SCHEMES
Variations of one color

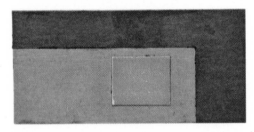

ADJACENT SCHEMES
Neighbor colors

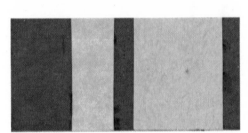

COMPLEMENTARY SCHEMES
Opposite colors
The second and third
rectangles of color on page 71 are also
good complementary harmonies.

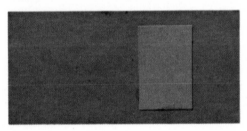

green combination is the red berries and dark, waxy green leaves of holly. These colors are shown above.

When complementary colors are seen together in nature, the effect is generally harmonious. Hues of spec-

trum intensity don't often appear together. Almost always one of the colors is neutralized or reduced in intensity, and appears as a soft shade or tone.

The orange and blue pair of complements is frequently seen. Look for it in a sunset, or in autumn leaves against the sky. You'll see it in advertisements and show windows, and you might even find it on the breakfast table, with orange juice, toast, and cereal on a blue cloth.

Look for examples of complementary colors that belong together. Experiment with the colors again, and try a few of your own. You'll find that one of the colors will need to be neutralized or toned down.

Tips on Color Harmony

You have read about only a few of the possibilities for selecting colors that belong together. It might be a good idea to review some of the things you learned in this chapter.

1. Beware of combinations of two or more intense colors. They are not likely to get on well together.

2. Use intense colors in small areas. Brilliant colors in large areas are likely to overwhelm the other colors.

3. Decide on the type of harmony or scheme you want before you begin work. Do you want it to be bold and exciting? Delicate? Quiet? Noisy? Plan your colors accordingly. And be sure to try it on the eye!

EXPERIENCES IN APPRECIATION

1. Select pieces of colored paper and try them together. Remember which kinds of colors seem to belong together, and which do not.

2. Arrange a series of color schemes on the bulletin board. The class may decide which are the best combinations.

3. Collect samples of fabrics. Try to find both plain and patterned samples. Combine them to make pleasing combinations. Two or three people can put the fabrics together, and the rest of the class may comment.

4. Try the experiments described in the first problem under Creative Activities. It requires the use of paint, but no particular skill. Anyone can enjoy experimenting with colors.

CREATIVE ACTIVITIES

1. Use water colors to experiment with various color combinations. Don't try to make a picture of anything. Let the colors flow together in interesting arrangements.

2. Experiment with colors to express emotions and moods, and your feelings on certain special occasions. For example, you might choose reds, yellows, and purples in bold brush strokes to express anger. Which colors would you use for serenity? National holidays suggest special colors. Which colors would you choose for Independence Day?

3. Discuss in class some ideas that might be expressed in color. Try some of these in free design form.

4. Paint some pictures in which the colors help to make the meaning clear. Express different moods in your paintings. Refer to the painting on page 193. Also to the one on page 186.

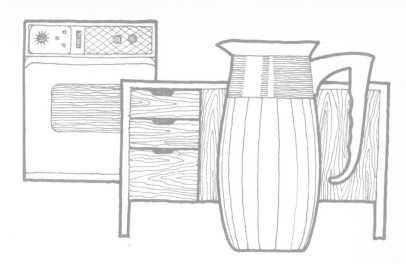

Chapter Six | Art Goes into Business

Do you recall your discovery of pleasing forms in trees, water, and clouds, and the many fine "designs" in animals? Remember some of the ways color is used to produce certain results? You may ask, "Well, what does all this lead up to?" You might say it's just a way to have more fun. Or you may decide that each of the things you studied had a meaning for some future use. Be on the watch for beauty in art and nature everywhere.

Perhaps you have thought that each chapter in this book deals with a separate form of art. Yet learning about design and color from different approaches leads to better choice of clothing, or points out how to improve your ideas in home decorating. Your knowledge of color and design helps you to decide which combinations are the right ones. As you begin to observe things around you in a new, fresh way, you

also begin to discriminate between the ordinary and the fine. This is called development of taste. The development of good taste is the result of all your art experiences. Good taste means that your choices fit your needs, please others, and give long satisfaction.

Manufacturers know about the development of good taste, too. They hire artists to design their products so people will approve them. How often have you said, "Oh, I like that. It looks good!" You may be speaking of a watch, a record player, a box of cereal, or an automobile! You like these things first of all for their appearance. In Chapter 2 you read about the industrial designer who designs automobiles. He might also design electric toasters, refrigerators, or chairs, as well as the other items listed above. So you see, art really "goes into business." This chapter shows you how.

Let Art Sell It

Let's suppose a manufacturer has produced a line of well-designed toasters, ladders, or chairs. Now he must market them. This is where the smart businessman says, "Let art sell it!" You can readily see that the artist plays a big part here. He designs posters, circulars, signs, and advertising layouts for magazines and newspapers. He creates animated TV commercial art and "stage settings."

Here again, good taste is important, since we know that the chief purpose of an advertisement is to catch the attention of the reader and persuade him to buy the product. Many advertisers do not know that it's easier to attract attention and make a favorable impression by emphasizing one center of interest through orderly arrangements than to crowd as many things as possible into a limited space. You can easily make a comparison of a simple, orderly arrangement with a crowded, cluttered one. Next time you walk through a shopping district, look at the display windows of several stores along the street. You're sure to see some uncluttered, tastefully arranged displays. And close by, you're certain to see some which appear to be a hodge-podge of all the items in the store! The owner of this latter store doesn't realize that such a condition of disorder serves only to confuse the passerby. The store owner who carefully and tastefully displays only "lead" items is actually telling the shopper that there are many more fine things inside, displayed as handsomely as those in the window. This is a subtle invitation to come in and look for them.

In some instances, it is better not to use any advertising. If an advertisement creates a bad impression, it is not likely to persuade people to buy. Compare the highways on the next page for beauty. Obviously the upper one is far more attractive than the other, which is marred by ugly signboards. People who enjoy driving through beautiful country on good roads cannot help but be annoyed by billboards which mar and interfere with the landscape. They will not be persuaded to buy products advertised on billboards which destroy the natural beauty of the countryside.

Packages Sell the Products

Just above, you read that the purpose of advertising is to catch the attention of the reader and persuade him to buy the product. Do you agree that the product may be its own best advertisement? Isn't this true of automobiles? Wouldn't it also apply to furniture, household appliances, or a box of cereal? A product advertises itself by its appearance. No matter how many words we might write about something, if it's not good looking, people don't want it. Have you ever looked closely at the boxes, envelopes, and packages that contain products you or your parents buy? Many of these are planned with great care. A well designed, attractively colored package suggests a high quality product inside. Some products are identified by their package designs. Which brands of breakfast cereal can you identify by the package design?

Packages of the future may be quite different from those of today. New materials will increase the possibilities for greater beauty and utility alike. On page 86 are pictured three delightful new package designs made of aluminum foil and strong paper. These packages do not appear to be billboards-in-miniature, as others often do. Created by a group of industrial designers,

these sparkling containers encourage a prospective buyer to select their contents purely because of the beauty and usefulness of the package.

The attractive containers in the top photo are for dry products, such as candy, soap powder, or perhaps salt, in the smaller size. These curved and fluted drum containers allow for perforations or a turn top for dispensing contents. The tripod containers shown below them are well suited for milk or soft drinks. Picture your milk served in this clever style. Now do you see how a well designed package can "catch on?"

PENNSYLVANIA TURNPIKE COMMISSION

COURTESY NATIONAL ROADSIDE COUNCIL

85

The container below is a fascinating cube which separates into six individual modular, or similar, pyramids. It might be useful for ice cream, or perhaps cheese, with the package dividing into six servings. How would you like to serve ice cream to your friends in this manner? Just peel back those sides and dig in! Choose your favorite flavor by the color of the section! Let's see now, cream-yellow foil for vanilla, green for mint—you supply the others!

An attractive container need not be elaborately designed. In fact, some of the best designed containers suit their purposes so well we hardly notice them. But we always have something to say about containers or cups that *don't*

ALUMINUM COMPANY OF AMERICA

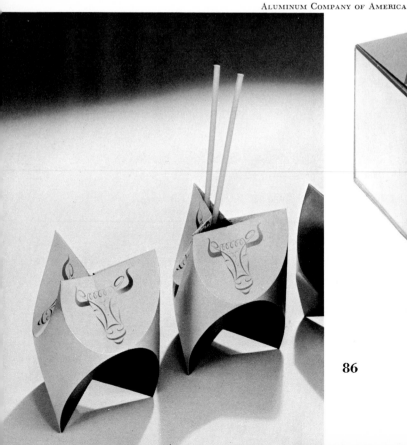

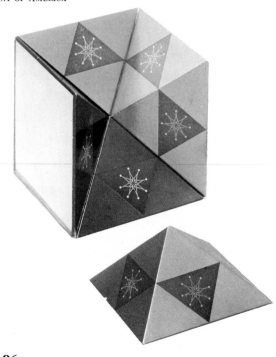

work well. How often have you noticed people juggling paper cups of hot coffee? The insulated cup pictured below eliminates this problem. The strong rim helps to hold the cup in shape and makes it easy to drink from too. What can you say about the proportions of this cup? Would it tip over easily, or does it sit solidly on the table?

Choose a day when each member of the class will bring the most interesting package he can find. Discuss the attractive and functional qualities in each of these containers.

Designs in All Sizes

The industrial designer may be commissioned to design or redesign any product from very small to very large. The examples shown here give some idea of the many thousands of products the industrial designer may be called upon to create or improve.

Have you ever really looked at the water fountain in your school? Is it well proportioned, clean in line, and attractive in color? In other words, is it well designed? The fountain pictured here fits that description. Even the water outlet is attractively designed, and its simple lines make it easy to clean and leaves no hidden place for germs.

Not so long ago the telephone was a tall, strange-looking instrument with a mouthpiece at the top, a receiver hooked along the side, and a flat base

SCOTT PAPER CO.

HAWS DRINKING FAUCET CO.

on which it stood. But see what happened! The designer took the same basic instrument and combined the mouthpiece and receiver into a single unit that comfortably fits the hand. He then angled both ends of the unit so that one end fits snugly against your ear, while the other is close to your mouth. The entire instrument is enclosed in a smooth, compact, well proportioned case. Have you ever thought how important a role the designer played in developing the modern telephone?

Many homes today have record changers, tape recorders, and stereophonic amplifiers and speakers. A few years ago these items were often housed in individual box sections that were stacked as neatly and inconspicuously as possible in an out-of-the-way place, or they were built into a massive cabinet that hid all the parts. The photo on this page illustrates how the designer has made these same parts fit into handsome and functional furniture units. You certainly wouldn't hide these in a

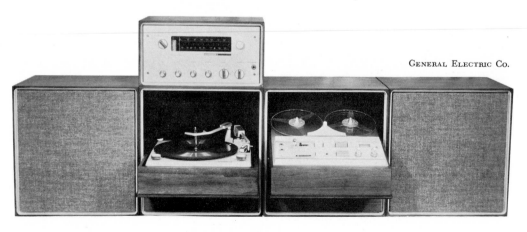

corner. On the contrary, you could well make them the center of interest in a game room or even a living room. Can you picture these units on a long, low bench, or on a shelf?

Other designers have placed record players in cabinets that blend well with other furniture. An important part of the cabinet shown below is the space for record storage. Where do you keep your records? How could you improve upon your record storage?

Many industrial designers are engaged in designing furniture. This is because furniture must be "just right" in order to sell. Do you recall how carefully your parents go about selecting a chair or a table? Of course, it has to be something they like and can afford. They want all the family to like it, but this isn't all. It must be comfortable, look well in the house, and do the special job for which it is selected. The chest pictured on page 90 would fit these requirements for many people. Like much other contemporary furniture, it is clean-lined and well proportioned. It is specifically designed to

JENS RISOM DESIGN, INC.

give maximum storage. The spacing of shelves and drawers practically eliminates waste space. The many compartments allow you to store clothing neatly and to find your garments without a lot of hunting. The designer can help to make a home more orderly and comfortable in many ways.

The photo of the chess set on page 91 is still another example of fine de-sign. Made of aluminum, these chess-men are a most attractive addition to a game room. Clean line, good proportion, and an attractive surface finish are as important to the chess set as to a telephone, a chest of drawers, or an automobile. Remember that appearance comes first when considering the purchase of a product. The successful designer is aware of this!

In our study of color in Chapter 5 we examined a photo of rug patterns. This photo is on page 75. The artist who designed these rugs made use of the same art principles mentioned above—good proportion, clean line, and even an attractive surface finish. However, he used these elements to create a design in color on a flat surface. Don't you agree that the results are extraordinary?

Art and Function

We have used the term "functional" a number of times in describing a product or article. If a product is functional, it satisfies the purpose for which it was created. But how does the designer combine function with elements of good design? Remember that the designer must create a product that will be readily accepted by discriminating people. That's what he is paid for. Functional means *serving a purpose;*

therefore the designer must combine his elements so that the product will fulfill its purpose in the best manner possible. We might be able to cut into a tender steak with a plastic knife blade, but steel does the job better. A soft wood handle on a butcher knife might be comfortable to hold, but hard wood or plastic is just as comfortable and will last much longer. The aluminum chessmen below could not be made of wood in the same shapes, since they might easily be broken. By these examples we see that metal, glass, plastics, and other materials have different properties; the designer must select the one that best suits the purpose or function of the product, then create a design that is suited to the material he selects. He knows that wood is easily used in flat areas or soft curves, that metal pieces may be sharply curved or thin, that plastic can be molded and made in many

AUSTIN ENTERPRISES

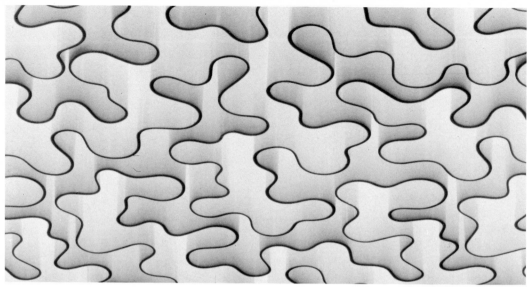

LUMINOUS CEILINGS, INC.

colors, and that cloth may be woven into intricate patterns.

Look for products that are functional and well designed. Bring pictures of these to class. Have a class discussion about functional design of automobiles, airplanes, furniture.

Some interesting examples of imaginative and functional uses for materials are shown on pages 86 and 87. The photograph above shows how plastic can be easily shaped to meet a special requirement. It shows a plastic ceiling that is installed below overhead lights. The curved plastic strips control the amount of light that shows through. This luminous ceiling is both attractive and functional.

On page 93 you see several examples of how aluminum sheets can be pierced, expanded, and pressed into useful and attractive screens and coverings. These sheets are widely used in architecture, both inside and outside of buildings.

Can you think of some uses for these aluminum sheets? Describe some examples of metal sheets or screens used in modern buildings. What uses could be made of these materials in and around the home? Fencing? Patio screening? For the fireplace?

Emphasis Says "Look!"

The chief importance of an advertisement is to catch the attention of the public and tell about a product or service. To do this, the advertisement must be emphatic or forceful.

You will recall the way colors can almost be made to shout for attention. The first color rectangle on page 69 does just that.

Advertisements can be made forceful or eye-catching in other ways. Many companies use a "softer" approach, over and over again. For example, look at the trademarks on page 94. Millions of people have seen these on television and in magazines, and can identify them at once. These are only a few of the many identifying marks used by industries throughout the world. You can probably think of several others. They are advertisements themselves, and have been carefully designed to cause instant recognition.

Find other trademarks that identify companies you know about. Be prepared to discuss a few of these in class. Are the designs complicated or simple? Are they unique—that is, different from all others? Which ones are more easily recognized, and why?

Stop!—And Read

When we look through a magazine today we may browse from cover to cover and stop to examine only a few pages. While a large part of the magazine may be devoted to advertisements, only a few advertising pages tell us to "Stop!—and read." We stop because there is something about these ads that separates them from the others. The most important thing is that they are different. Second, they look interesting enough to make us take time to read the copy.

The advertising artist is hired to tell a story in graphic form, to tell the prospective buyer that this is a product

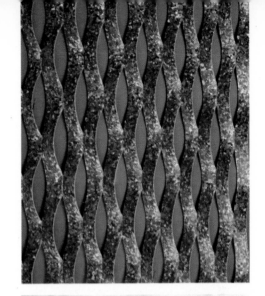

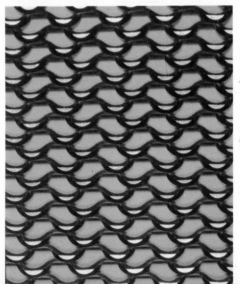

93

he needs, that it is better than its competitors. His success depends upon whether his advertising design is better than that of a competitor.

The design on page 95 is a success! It combines eye-catching appeal with well proportioned layout. The illustration matches the copy, "Infinite Uniformity." You may notice also that the blocks of copy below the illustration suggest infinite uniformity as well.

Some advertisers use the same picture, or the same kind of picture, several times, so that the public gets to know the product by recognizing the "ad." No matter what kind of emphasis the advertiser uses, his goal is the same — to make the reader take notice.

SCOTT PAPER COMPANY

A Sampling of Posters

The posters illustrated on pages 96 and 97 are examples of effective advertising design. The artists have made them better than ordinary by combining art elements with personal appeal. Comments accompany the examples. They will help you to understand what makes these posters outstanding, and to recognize outstanding qualities in others you will see in magazines, newspapers, billboards, and packages.

Emphasis Is a Principle of Art

Art arrangements built around a center of interest are usually more successful than those which lack such a center. This principle, called *emphasis*, is important in all kinds of art. It will help you to plan a poster, arrange a room, or paint a picture. It will also help you think of the most important thing in your arrangement.

Advertising and Emotion

You may wonder how these two words, advertising and emotion, are related. But if you realize that your feelings about things are really emotions, you will see how an advertisement "uses" them. The ad on page 98 shows how the artist makes our emotions work to help sell the idea or product. This was designed for a television series titled, "I Remember Mama." The artist's task was to create a desire in the reader to watch the

INFINITE
UNIFORMITY

Purity and gage uniformity are just two of the many characteristics of Alcoa® Aluminum Foil that lead to greater life expectancy and more dependable performance for capacitors. Alcoa's exacting quality controls in every step of manufacturing result in a foil which meets the highest performance needs of the capacitor industry.

Alcoa can furnish a complete range of gages and alloys for every type of capacitor foil from subminiature electrolytics used in missiles and rockets to oil-filled paper types used on power transmission lines.

Alcoa has developed methods of controlling the quality and performance characteristics for the various types of capacitors for specific applications. To insure the quality of its electrolytic foil, for example, Alcoa etches, forms and measures capacitance and other electrical characteristics on each lot of foil. This assures delivery of a product capable of developing and maintaining consistently high capacitance.

Where and how can Alcoa's research and development team help you with your design problems? Contact your nearest Alcoa sales office for complete details or write Aluminum Company of America, 1701-H Alcoa Building, Pittsburgh 19, Penna.

The Weekly World! This is the name of the newspaper which is rolled into a megaphone shape. The meaning is at once clear, broadcasting the news in dramatic fashion. What more could a poster say?

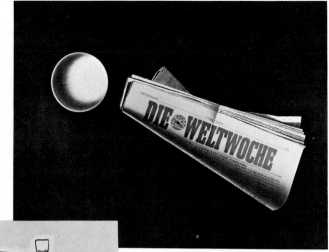

Made in France, but you know what it means even without words — just the name of the product and a man with a very sensitive nose!

Production will win the war. The strong hand of America's manpower is symbolized in this poster. It calls for direct action — now! Strong contrasts give strength to the design.

96

This poster forcefully describes the function of a subway advertisement. People who are in a hurry won't notice a "quiet" poster. Stop 'em with a powerful design —strong contrast and bright color.

GIFT OF THE ARTIST

With bright colors and a suggestion of interesting sights to be seen, this invitation to travel by air is a good one.

GIFT OF THE ARTIST

A trio of smaller posters. They are attractively designed notices of scheduled performances and exhibitions. How do they differ from notices you have seen?

COLLECTION, THE MUSEUM OF MODERN ART, NEW YORK

programs. This he accomplished by appealing to emotion, using the rocking chair, knitting basket, and footstool, things which the reader recognized as belonging to "Mama." The emotion is sentiment. Recalled to mind are the many enjoyable times the reader had with "Mama," perhaps watching her make candy, or helping her wrap sandwiches for a family picnic. This advertisement is actually aimed at the age level of your mothers and fathers, so the "Mama" referred to here is your grandmother! But look at the picture again. Can you feel what it's saying to you? Would you like to see a program based on your mother's times — the 1940's and '50's, or her earlier years, the '20's and '30's?

Color Can Make or Break

The right color is most important in making an advertisement pleasing and emphatic. It has been proved by scientific investigation that some color combinations can be seen at much greater distance than others. Black letters on a yellow background can be read further than any other combination of colors. Yellow light rays have greater penetrating power than any other. That is why center lines on highways in some states are painted yellow instead of white.

PITTSBURGH CORNING CORPORATION AGENCY, KETCHUM, McLEOD & GROVE, INC.

Of course, we don't want to use only black and yellow. But it is important that colors have enough contrast to be seen and read easily. When choosing colors for an advertisement, think first of the conditions involved. If your advertisement is to be read from a distance, choose colors that are legible from a distance. If the advertisement is to be read close at hand, then more subtle color combinations may be used. Be certain to choose colors that are harmonious. Good color combinations are pleasant, and they make good impressions. Unpleasant color combinations will not make a good impression, and people will not be persuaded to buy. The study of color in Chapter 5 should help you think of many color combinations that are both legible and compatible.

Color Photographs in Advertising

Sometimes the advertiser wants the observer to see his product in its true color and in a real setting. The advertisement may then be made from a color photograph. This is a very expensive process, so the advertiser who uses it attempts to make the reader see his product in the best possible setting.

Sometimes an advertiser crowds too many things into one layout, and the refinement that he might get with color is lost. Other advertisers know that a carefully planned color ad can be very complimentary to their products. This often means using few colors, selected to suggest quality and good taste. The advertisement back on page 75 is a fine example of careful color selection, lending an air of high status to the product. The distinguished, well dressed gentleman looking over the selection is obviously interested only in the very best! His sophistication and expensive good taste suggest that these rugs are truly "collector's" items. Have you noticed the background color? This soft gray tone was probably the most thoughtfully selected color in the scene. Can you tell why? Why are the walls and floor the same color?

There are two things about this advertisement you should notice especially: (1) Take note of the restraint used in the selection of colors. Did you realize that only two colors are used in the rugs? They are red and orange, in various intensities and values. Black is used here and there for contrast. The artist knew that by selecting only a few colors, the reader could fully appreciate their subtle differences. Actually, this is another form of emphasis, isn't it? (2) Note the unusual arrangement. Hanging the rugs on the wall draws attention to them because this is not the way we usually see rugs. Remember these points. Look for similar examples in other advertisements. Look for unusual displays in store windows.

Do you think closely related colors (adjacents) or opposite colors make the best effect on posters? Why or why not?
Do you think a combination of light and dark values or light and middle values makes a more legible combination? Why?

Study Your Newspaper and Magazine Advertisements

There are a great many advertisements in our newspapers and magazines. The purpose of each advertisement is to sell a product or an idea, but some of them are more successful than others. Readers of newspapers and magazines do not have time to read all advertisements. We know that they read only those which attract their attention and are easy to read. Try an experiment. Take a magazine which has several pages of advertising and turn through the pages without looking for any special thing. Which advertisements caught your eye and interested you enough so that you read the whole advertisement? Next ask several members of your class to do the same thing. How many of you noticed the same advertisements? You will probably find that the same advertisements are forceful enough to catch attention.

Next analyze these advertisements and try to find out why they caught your attention. Do you find a successful use of art principles: emphasis, pleasing proportions, and orderly arrangement?

Collect newspaper and magazine advertisements. Select those which you consider the most effective. Analyze each one for the use of art principles. For example, in your opinion which ones shows the best use of the principle of emphasis? The most effective use of color?

Good Lettering Is Important

Nearly all advertisements carry at least a few words, and the lettering in these words can do a great deal to make the advertisement forceful and attractive. If the lettering is poor, it may make the poster both ugly and hard to read. On the other hand, if the lettering is good, it makes the poster more attractive and easier to understand.

Sometimes an advertisement is made

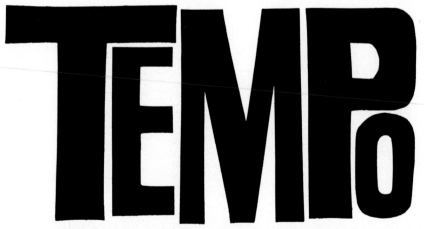

ATlantic 1-0980-81-82 Granite Building, 6th & Wood, Pittsburgh 22, Pennsylvania

up of lettering alone. This can be very interesting or very dull, depending upon how inventive the artist is. Letters can be grouped to form designs, or their shapes changed so that they fit together as a unit. Of course, the style of lettering must suit the use for which it is intended. The name plate on page 100 is a good example of lettering used to create an interesting and eye-catching design. This design was used to advertise a commercial art studio. Striking contrasts attract the reader's attention. The interesting sizes and shapes along with the lively arrangement of the letters make this an outstanding example of lettering design.

Now You Try It!

Everyone should know how to make good printed letters in at least one style of alphabet. There are many occasions in anyone's life when it is handy to know how to letter a few words. You may need this skill for your maps and diagrams in other school subjects. There are frequent uses for lettering. At the beginning of this book we said that it is not necessary for everyone to draw well in order to understand and enjoy art. However, lettering is one kind of technical work that does not require great art talent. If you wish, you can learn to do good lettering.

Styles of Alphabets

Here are a few styles of alphabets with which you should become familiar. The simplest style is shown

Clean and NEAT LINE BOLD SIGN! ABCD

above. It is a single-line alphabet that is suitable for use in lettering maps, charts, diagrams, and small posters. In this style of alphabet each line is made with a single stroke of the pen or pencil that makes a thin line. However, for posters or signs it is best to use a heavy crayon or pen with a broad, flat nib. Some flat-nibbed pens have very broad disks, and these are especially suitable for lettering signs or posters quickly. Oversize letters are often drawn first, then filled in. The professional artist uses a very light guideline, then paints his letters directly onto the poster board. He may use chalk or light pencil lines so that he can make changes easily. With some prac-

101

tice you can make clean-looking block letters such as shown on page 101. Why don't you try? This kind of letter looks best when it's quite large. Often these letters are drawn first and then transferred to the poster.

Another style of alphabet with which you should be familiar is a very old one. It was first used by the Romans on their great monuments, and so it is known as the Roman alphabet. The letters were first drawn on the stone and then cut with a chisel. A great many modern alphabets are patterned after this old Roman alphabet. Sometimes the letters are made with lines varying in thickness and with different proportions, but they are based on the Roman style. Most of our books are printed with a style of alphabet derived from the Roman.

ABCD

This style of alphabet is not used for quick lettering because the letters must be carefully drawn and correctly proportioned. This alphabet is printed where elegance or formality is desirable, such as on important documents. It is sometimes used in advertising to lend an air of refinement and dependability to a product or service.

Beauty in the Printed Page

While we are discussing beauty in letter forms, we should also think of beauty in the printed page. Letters should not only have beautiful forms, but should also be arranged well on the page. Good spacing between letters, between words, between paragraphs, and in the margins is of the utmost importance in securing a fine effect.

The arrangement made with blocks of letters and surrounding spaces should be thought of as page design. You know that people are more apt to be impressed by simply designed, well arranged displays than by cluttered, carelessly arranged ones. How can this knowledge help you in your written schoolwork? Look at the page layout on pages 96 and 97. These pages are tastefully arranged, well proportioned.

Greetings to Friends

Christmas, New Year's, Valentine's Day, Easter, birthdays—these are times to send greetings to your friends. Every year the people of the United States send millions of greeting cards as tokens of good wishes. Most of these cards are inexpensive. But even they may be very attractive. Your special problem in buying greeting cards is to select those cards which say in the best possible way what you want them to say. Here again, study of art will help.

What's the Occasion?

You have studied the principles of art in designing automobiles, in advertisements, and in painting. Those same principles apply to selection of greeting cards. You'll be more satisfied

"Silent Night," by Joseph Hirsch.

103

with cards that are well proportioned and show good taste in color selection. But another principle is involved which you must consider first of all: Greeting cards are designed to suit a special occasion. For instance, Christmas cards generally include such ideas as Christmas trees, churches, angels, winter landscapes, Santa Claus and his reindeer, or the Mother and Child. Many people prefer to send cards which suggest the origin of the celebration of Christmas—Christ's birthday. The card pictured on page 103 is based on this theme. It is a scene in a big city on Christmas Eve. A star gleams on a giant Christmas tree and a pale moon shines through the snowy night. Two people, alone in the park, gaze in wonder and reverence at the scene on this holy night. In this Christmas card the artist has created an interpretation of the famous Christmas song, "Silent Night."

Sometimes you may have to choose a card for someone who is confined by illness or an accident but is not in desperate condition. Such a person needs to be cheered up! Card companies make a line of cartoon cards especially for this purpose. Because these cards are funny, they help the ailing person to make light of his burden, whatever it may be. It is a common belief that one feels better if he can smile at his own ills. The cleverly drawn illustration on page 105 is accompanied inside by the lines, "What some people won't do for attention!" Don't you

think that this whimsical, sparkling drawing and snappy remark would have an effervescent effect on the patient? Have you ever received a funny get-well card?

When you choose a card for the invalid, you have a special purpose in mind—to make him forget his troubles or ills for awhile. There are other occasions when you might wish to use cartoon cards, too. How about Valentine's Day, or a special birthday greeting to someone who likes a joke? You might try a humorous Mother's Day card. It works!

Make Your Own

Many people enjoy making their own Christmas cards, valentines, or other greeting cards. It is a good hobby. There are different ways of making them and you will enjoy trying different methods. Cards can be drawn and painted. This means that each card must be done separately, so if you wish to make several it may require too much time.

Another method of making greeting cards is with a linoleum print. There is not space in this book to tell you all about how to do this, but you can find out about it by consulting the books listed in the bibliography at the end of this book. Your teacher will be able to help you. The process, explained briefly, is this: A piece of linoleum the size and shape of the card is secured. The pattern is drawn upon the block. Parts of the block are cut away so that the

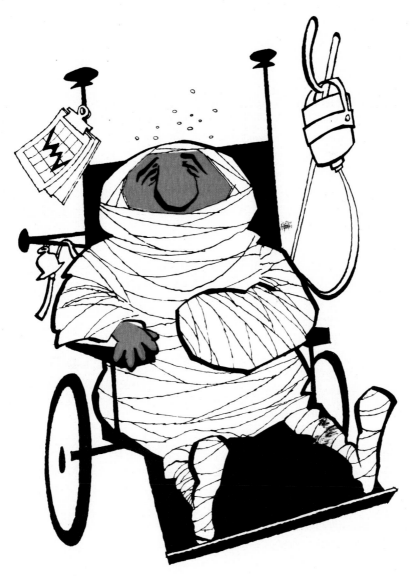

HALLMARK CARDS, INC.

block can be used to print the pattern on the cards. In this way a number of cards can be made quickly from one block. If you plan to make linoleum-print Christmas cards, remember that the design should be very simple, with no fine lines and as little lettering as possible. Letters are hard to cut.

Very attractive cards can be made by paper cutting—colored papers are cut and pasted with charming effects.

You may wonder how the cards sold in the stores are made. An artist makes the original drawing and colors it. This is sent to an engraver who makes line engravings (called "cuts") or color plates. These are used for printing many thousands of cards on a printing press. Your drawing could be used to make a plate from which thousands of cards could be printed, but it would be expensive.

EXPERIENCES IN APPRECIATION

1. Report to your class any examples of how art sells an article—in other words, how an advertisement catches the attention of the public and persuades it to buy.

2. Collect advertisements of many kinds—folders, cards, posters, signs, and others. From these advertisements select the ones which do the best job of selling. Explain your choices.

3. Study other styles of alphabets and collect samples. You will find other styles of alphabets shown in the reference books listed at the end of this book.

4. Arrange for a criticism lesson on greeting cards. First collect some greeting cards. Put them in a pile and let each member of the class select one. Each person will criticize his card for the following points: (Remember that criticism includes good points as well as bad points.)

    a. Suitability of idea.

    b. Treatment or character.

    c. Lettering.

Arrange a bulletin-board exhibition of good greeting cards just before the day on which they are intended to be used.

CREATIVE ACTIVITIES

1. Design and paint a poster for a school activity. Make use of the principles of advertising discussed in this chapter. Refer to the examples on pages 96 and 97.

2. Design a greeting card for a special occasion. Remember that a personal greeting is most appreciated. Use ink with a water color wash, or a linoleum block.

3. Letter some simple signs, using the flat-nibbed pens.

Chapter Seven	# Figures and Faces

This book is a search for beauty in any form that may chance to cross your path. You have found it in automobiles, animals, trees, and advertisements—sometimes in objects made by man, sometimes in nature. This search must include a study of the human figure. Artists have always seen beauty in the human body. Figures and faces have long intrigued painters and sculptors. Some authorities believe that the finest art is a representation of the human form. Some statues and paintings of the human figure and face are very beautiful and rightfully have become famous. In this chapter you will become acquainted with some of these famous works of art.

Figures and faces are also depicted in cartoons and caricatures. A caricature is a kind of drawing in which there is an exaggeration of certain outstanding features. Later on in this chapter

you will look at some of these drawings and decide how important they are in representations of the human form.

Strength in Face and Figure

You can quickly identify the forceful lines and strong forms in the statue illustrated on page 108. This great statue, "Victory of Samothrace," was made by a sculptor who recognized strength of line and form in the human figure, and who was able to transfer what he saw into marble. The ancient Greeks used a single female figure with wings to symbolize victory. The "Victory of Samothrace" was meant to commemorate a great naval victory, when the Greeks defeated the Egyptian fleet, about 306 B.C. There are no historical records to tell what happened to it since the time of the ancient Greeks. The head and arms have been broken off and lost forever. Probably the hands

Left: This famous Greek statue called "The Victory of Samothrace" is an excellent example of beautiful rhythmic line. Right: "Mask of Anna Pavlova," by Malvina Hoffman.

held a trumpet upon which the Victory played the song of triumph. The pedestal was shaped like the prow of a boat. Can you see this great figure with sweeping wings standing as though it faced the wind as the boat cut through the water? Even without the head and arms, it is an exciting sculpture. The swinging lines of the draperies and wings, and the smooth strong forms of the body visible between the folds create a figure of both beauty and power. Modern sculptors rarely include as much detail in their work. They emphasize simple forms, or the essential masses and movements. But a sculpture more inspiring and more powerful than "Victory of Samothrace" would be hard to find.

Another splendid example of strength in form is the "Mask of Anna Pavlova," pictured above, by the great American woman sculptor Malvina Hoffman. The mask is done in wax, which permits delicate carving in the headpiece and details of the features. The fine curves in the arch of the eyebrows, the mouth, the nostrils, and the strong contours of the whole face suggest enduring strength. The artist was successful, for she certainly intended her mask to have an enduring quality, just as the memory of Pavlova, a famous ballerina, will live among lovers of ballet. The movement of line and form in this head is not as exciting as in the "Victory of Samothrace," but is just as beautiful in another way.

The very old and famous picture below shows us how artists of the fifteenth century pictured figures and faces. It's an excellent example of the richly decorated and symbolic subjects that were popular for painting. The flowing lines and repeated curves are carefully placed to create a feeling of continuous and graceful movement. As you look at this painting, your eye is led from figure to figure, around and between, until you find yourself among them, examining the many details that catch your eye.

The painting was made by Sandro Botticelli, an Italian painter who lived during the period of history when Columbus discovered America. He completed this picture nearly twenty years before Columbus made his first voyage to America. You see, artists have understood the beauty of the human figure for many centuries. It is called "Spring" and is a symbolic representation of the spring season. Slender, graceful figures in a forest glade celebrate the coming of the spring. It is fanciful and charming with its fairylike figures, flying cherub, and spring flowers.

A very fine example of beautiful line is found in the marble bust called

This famous painting called "Spring," by Botticelli symbolizes the elegance so admired in the 15th century.

"Maidenhood," page 111, by a modern American sculptor, George Gray Barnard. The sweep of the hair drawn back over the neck, the delicate profile, the tilt of the head, and the smooth curves of the shoulders produce a lovely sculpture. Its delicate line and clean surfaces suggest a pure and beautiful person.

Action Creates Strong Movement

You have seen that the lines in the human figure may be harmonious. When the body is thrown into action required by running, jumping, diving, skating, or throwing, the lines or movement are greatly emphasized. Artists know this and sometimes portray the human figure in a strong action pose. One of the most famous statues in the world, made by an ancient Greek sculptor, Myron, shows an athlete in full action as he hurls the discus, page 111. The discus is the heavy plate which he holds in his right hand. He whirls about to gain force before making the throw. Myron caught the action of the figure just before the arm swings forward. The figure stands firmly, and is full of strong movement. Note the swing of the line from the right hand down over the shoulders, down the left arm, and on down the bent leg. Then notice the strong line starting at the head and sweeping down the right side of the body and right leg. The statue is dramatic in the way it expresses movement.

There are many athletic activities in which the body performs fine, rhythmic movements. As you watch swimmers, runners, or skaters, you see these movements come and go. When the artist captures the sense of motion in stone or paint, he creates a kind of beauty that everyone enjoys. Running is especially concerned with swift movement. Artists have frequently chosen a runner for a subject, for this very reason.

Fine Proportions in the Human Figure

Most persons are so familiar with the general appearance of the human figure that they do not often think of how beautiful its proportions can be. The sculptor must know a great deal about proportions in the human figure. He knows the proportions of all the parts in relation to others, such as height in relation to the length of the head and the thickness and width of the chest, waist, and hips. Sometimes he tries to create a statue that is ideal in proportions. Many art authorities feel that the sculptors of ancient Greece were most successful in creating human figures with beautiful and ideal proportions. Certainly the figure of "The Discus Thrower" is splendid in its proportions. The Greek sculptors created many statues of athletes, giving them nearly perfect human figures. For this reason, many of the figures could have been brothers, even twins!

Many artists and sculptors prefer to represent things as they exist. A good

A marble bust called "Maidenhood,"
by George Gray Barnard.

"The Discus Thrower," made by the
Greek sculptor, Myron, more than
2,000 years ago.

A statue by Malvina Hoffman representing a Blackfoot Indian of the western plains.

example of a realistic figure is the Indian pictured on this page. Lean-bodied and hard-muscled, this suntanned brave appears very much alive. This sculpture was made by Malvina Hoffman, who also made the mask of Anna Pavlova mentioned near the start of this chapter. It is meant to represent a typical Blackfoot Indian of the western plains. It stands in the Hall of Man in the Field Museum, Chicago.

Remember that Greek sculptors tried to make their statues with ideal rather than realistic proportions. It often happened that a fine athlete was too muscular in the arms, legs, or chest. But a statue in his honor would show his figure in ideal proportions. The Indian is quite realistic, and looks even a little hungry.

Portraits in Stone and Paint

What is the purpose of a good portrait? Does it show only how a person looks, or should it do something more?

A good portrait is a good likeness and much more. It shows character and personality, or in other words it tells what the person is like. A likeness shows whether you have a straight or turned-up nose, a square or pointed chin, and other things of this nature. But a real portrait tells something about what kind of a person you are: whether you are bold or timid, serious or fun-loving, and other traits.

By examining a few famous portrait studies in sculpture and painting, you

112

"The Laughing Cavalier," by Franz Hals. This portrait study shows character and personality.

can see how much they tell about character and personality. "The Laughing Cavalier," page 113, by Franz Hals, shows us a gentleman of the seventeenth century dressed in his Sunday-best costume. Don't you feel that he must be a bit vain, to wear such fancy clothes? Still, he is gay, bold, and dashing. Without a doubt he enjoys life greatly.

Now look at the painting on page 115. It was painted about 350 years ago by a Japanese artist named Kiyomasu I. This is an ink and paint portrait of a famous actor in Japan at that time. He is dressed here as a gay young man-about-town. His coat is elaborately decorated with calligraphic symbols, which can be translated into phrases like "white waves," "flower," and others. These might have been words from a song or popular story. We can see that this fellow was very proud of his beautifully decorated clothes, and he swaggered just a little as he walked along. The Japanese actor and the cavalier were both dashing gentlemen of their time.

The quaint-looking wood statue you see on page 116 is also a portrait, and it served as a house post under a native hut on New Zealand. It was made by the Maoris, who are the native inhabitants of this island country in the South Pacific. The flat head and strong legs suggest that this sturdy-looking young fellow might have held up a great amount of weight. The figure was carved from a section of tree trunk about three feet long. The fierce countenance and decorations on the figure are those of a warrior. This could be a warning to possible trespassers to stay away. One might suppose that the owner carved this statue to look like himself, or at least the way he wished to look to others! Every man thought of himself in a different way, so each house would display a different form of figure. A stranger might identify an occupant by studying the carvings for tribal rank or decorations. Judging from the house post illustrated here, this remarkable race of people developed a high degree of skill in decorative carving.

An equally interesting portrait is the Zapotec figure, page 117. Carved in clay, it probably represents one of the gods of this Indian tribe. The Zapotecs built a major civilization during ancient times in southern Mexico. Their artistry is evident in the remains of great temples, tombs, and stone slabs.

This awesome fellow, life-size or larger, would be a frightening sight to a simple tribesman. Would you like to meet him in a dark stone temple, with a fire throwing unearthly patterns of light and shadow on his face and figure? Why do you suppose the Zapotec sculptor pictured him this way?

Stories Come Alive

When you look at paintings, drawings, or sculptures of people, you often find out a great deal about the people. You wouldn't think the cavalier and the fierce Maori warrior could care very

An ink and paint portrait of a gay young Japanese man-about-town,
dressed in traditional costume.

115

much about what the other was doing. While the cavalier looked for excitement and diversion among elite social circles, the warrior must have had thoughts of protecting his family and providing the basic necessities of food and shelter in that primitive land. These works of art say something to us about the lives of the subjects. Most paintings and sculptures tell a story. Often it's a short story, and may be only in the mind of the artist, but other people who see it can usually tell the same story if they look carefully enough. Novels and short stories, poems, and even songs take on added meaning and realism when an artist interprets the words for the reader.

The lithograph on page 118, "Music Lesson," is a good example of storytelling. Thomas Hart Benton, an American artist who is famous for his pure Americana painting and drawing, tells a story of a hard working father and his little daughter. We can step into this farmhouse living room and enjoy the music lesson along with the little girl, just as if we were invited. The farmer's clothes, the oil lamp on the table, and the scrubbed board floor tell us much about the life of this family. What story can you tell from the painting?

"Serenade," Mervin Jules' portrait of a boy playing and singing for his girl, is a woodcut. The original is in two tones. Besides the black there is a background color, which appears gray in this reproduction. This boy's feet

A Maori house post of the 18th century. This is a self-portrait of a fierce warrior.

and relaxed attitude suggest that he's spent many hours playing the guitar, and the girl is fascinated by his ability. Practice makes perfect—or we can hope at least that it brings us closer. Can you tell anything else about this young musician? Look at page 119.

A woodcut is made by carving away the background, leaving only the lines to be printed. Ink is rolled onto the block, which is then pressed onto paper. Woodcuts, and linoleum block prints too, produce a pattern of lines that is quite different from drawings or paintings. The tool marks and simple printing method produce a rich surface finish unlike any other. This technique has been a favorite of artists for

"Music Lesson," by Thomas Hart Benton.

centuries, and was often used for illustrating books and manuscripts.

The self-portrait on page 120, by Erich Heckel, is also a woodcut. Here the cutting technique is bolder, showing broad areas of solid color and strong, dark lines. In "Serenade," the artist used fine lines and a variety of shades to create a delicate overall surface pattern. Heckel's "Self-Portrait" has been cut with wide strokes and a minimum of detail. Only the most important features are retained—the lean face, thoughtful and observant eyes, clasped hands. One can look at this portrait and believe that the subject is a man who thinks deeply, perhaps of religion, of fine writing, or of creating beautiful

"Serenade," by Mervin Jules.

119

"Self Portrait," by Erich Heckel.

120

"Intermezzo," by Georges Schreiber.

works of art. It's the portrait of a plain man, one devoted to his ideals, honest, and kind.

George Schreiber painted this picture of an orchestra taking a rest. Its title, "Intermezzo," is deceiving because only a few of the musicians are in their seats. An intermezzo is light entertainment between acts or serious music. In this case the entertainment is provided by the few remaining musicians playing random notes or tuning their instruments.

The picture you see on page 122 tells a story of children on an outing. Children are often the favorite subjects of artists. There is a simple reason for this. Painters, sculptors, and writers create works of art that reflect the things they find most interesting. And to a sensitive adult, what could be more interesting than children?

Emilio Sanchez, the artist who drew the little children skipping along the road, lived on Barbados, the easternmost island of the West Indies. The drawing, made with colored lithograph crayon, is as lively as the children themselves. There is excitement in the brilliant white pattern of the girls' dresses and the boys' short pants, and in the movement of legs and feet. The trees, too, come alive in the scene, as if they shared the pleasure of the day. The blue sky and sun-bright yellow and green fields in the original help tell the story of a happy day.

Cartoons and Funny Pictures

You have been studying figures and faces depicted in paintings and statues. At the beginning of the chapter it was stated that you would also study cartoons, and see how they represent the human form. But the cartoon does more than that. It also shows how people feel! Most cartoons are drawings of funny things that happen to people like you and me.

Nearly everyone likes the "funnies." We all like to laugh, and funny pictures can give us many chuckles. In this chapter we'll learn a little about what it is that makes them amusing.

There is a great deal of cartoon drawing in our modern world, so it is a good idea to learn to appreciate the best of it. Practically every newspaper and many magazines give space to funny pictures. Some magazines have cartoons on their covers, and some advertisers also use them. Cartoons appear frequently on the moving-picture screen. However, funny pictures are not new in the twentieth century. Cartoons have been found on the walls of the pharaohs' tombs in Egypt and on the walls of Roman buildings. But never in all history has there been so much cartoon drawing as today. If you

"Barbados Children," by Emilio Sanchez.

"Check," by William Gropper.

like to read the comic section in the Sunday newspaper, you can be glad that you did not live 100 years ago.

Clever Caricatures Are Amusing

Caricatures and cartoons alike exaggerate certain outstanding characteristics, but the caricature usually depicts someone real. On the other hand, the cartoon represents an idea.

Caricatures are really character studies. A clever artist not only can amuse us by exaggerating certain characteristics but also can show us something about character and personality. William Gropper, an American artist, is very good at this kind of drawing. In the picture above he has drawn two men seriously contemplating their game of chess. The almost smug expression of the man at the left indicates his pleasure at having gained an advantage. Do these men bring to mind anyone you know? What can you say about their clothing and their personalities?

This caricature is an etching, which means the picture was drawn on a coated metal plate. Acid was then used

123

"I can't understand why anyone who is as interested in food as you are doesn't want to learn to cook!"

AMERICAN MAGAZINE BY HARRY MACE

THE SATURDAY EVENING POST

"I don't play any of them. Over a period of years I've bought them from the kid next door."

to etch the lines into the metal. These lines hold the ink that is in turn transferred to the printing paper. The grays in the background are made by ink that was not wiped completely off the flat parts of the plate before printing. Each print is a little different from the others. (Prints made from the same woodcuts or linoleum blocks also show some variation.)

Some Cartoons Are "Joke Drawings"

Another type of funny picture is the cartoon in which there is a joke. There are many kinds of joke cartoons, just as there are many kinds of jokes. For instance, we laugh at something ridiculous and quite impossible, at something which is a predicament to others, something very unexpected, or something very exasperating to those involved but laughable to those who look on.

In the cartoon on this page, the joke is on the mother. She is baffled by her daughter's interest in food, and lack of interest in preparing it. Does this happen at your house?

The other cartoon is amusing because the man has solved his problem in such a very unusual and unexpected way. Clever drawing expresses the visitor's amazement at the collection of musical instruments which are decorations for the living room.

Cheer Up!

Comic cartoons can cheer you up because they are pictures of the funny side of life. But cartoons are often used to make light of things that are serious, or things that can be very troublesome in real life. A favorite trick of cartoonists is to find one small incident in real life and build a picture story around it. These artists have great fun during elections, poking fun at one candidate and then another. Also, they use incidents based on home life. These are popular because the subject matter is so familiar. Maybe the cartoonist is drawing you, or perhaps me! Has your mother ever scolded you for using a towel when your hands aren't clean, or

for tracking mud onto the kitchen floor? Whitney Darrow has made such an incident seem very funny. That is, you and I think it's funny. Mother may not appreciate the joke as much, particularly if this happened just after she cleaned the floor. Not many years ago you might have found yourself in this very picture. Has the cartoonist caught the lively mood of the two little cowboys?

The cartoon on page 126 demonstrates how an artist can exaggerate certain features and outstanding characteristics in a rather wild way. This cartoon makes fun of our desire to

125

NOT <u>THE</u> MAD BOMBER **!?!**

know important people. Compare the fussy, overdressed matron with the low-life, ragged character in this stovepipe hat. The woman is exclaiming, "Not THE mad bomber?!" Because she has read of him in the papers, she is obviously thrilled. The cartoonist drew this picture to make people laugh, yet there is a true basis for the idea.

Sometimes cartoons are drawn to illustrate current events, or to influence public opinion. These are called editorial cartoons. Some of them are humorous; others are strictly serious.

Many newspapers print editorial cartoons regularly.

Ideas Are Important

A joke drawing is not a success unless the idea back of it is really clever. No matter how good the drawing, the cartoon without a good idea is a failure. Cartoonists spend a great deal of time getting ideas. They have to watch what is going on in the world about them so they can make jokes about it. As you have seen, they may use very ordinary topics for their jokes.

Can you think of any clever ideas for cartoons? Try to find something in your own community for a joke drawing. Remember there are different ways of treating your idea. Use figures that could be anyone. Remember that a cartoon is funniest if it makes us think of something we have seen or done.

It is said that a good cartoon can express an idea more clearly and forcefully than ten times the amount of space in written words. Wouldn't you rather look at a clever cartoon than read a column of words?

Comic strips are examples of "reading" by pictures. Of course, they are often combinations of pictures and words, but how many more words would be necessary to tell the story without pictures?

Funny Pictures That Move

Everyone who watches television or goes to the movies is acquainted with funny pictures that move. Popeye, Tom Terrific, Bugs Bunny, Huckleberry Hound, Woody Woodpecker, and other amusing characters become very real and familiar to us. Have you noticed the way the newer characters are drawn? They are simpler, less "real," yet just as effective, aren't they? Famous tales such as Snow White have been animated in such a real manner that we are transferred to the land of make-believe.

The animation of drawings—which means adding motion to them—is one of the great developments in picture history. Animated cartoons made possible all sorts of amusing and fantastic effects which could not be produced in any other way. Smaller animals can throw elephants over a mountain range or uproot giant oak trees with the greatest of ease, flowers can bloom and wither in the period of a minute or two, fish can breathe out of water, or turtles can fly, if the cartoonist desires. Anything can happen. Color, music, and speech help make the cartoon amusing and delightful. Many of the effects are breathtakingly dramatic and beautiful, especially in full color.

Any feature-length animated cartoon requires thousands of separate drawings, photographed and arranged on a strip of film in successive order. When they are projected upon the screen, we see the drawings in such rapid succession that the characters appear to move their arms, legs, heads, and bodies—an animated cartoon.

Caricature in Painting

In order to express their ideas forcefully, by emphasizing or exaggerating certain features of a person or scene, some painters use caricature. "The Senate," on page 128, is a striking example of caricature in a painting. The senator, obviously saying very little with great gusto, is not getting much of a hearing in the nearly empty senate chamber. This picture says sarcastic things about our senate. We call this kind of art social satire.

"The Senate," by William Gropper.

Three-Dimensional Cartoons

Clever ideas by artists and designers are not limited to brush or pencil. The interesting figures on page 129 are really designs for chairs. A person simply walks up to one of these and sits down in its lap! The tall figure is a reclining chair which has been propped up just for the picture. Do you see why such chairs might be called three-dimensional cartoons? Where would you use these chairs?

We see many examples of three-dimensional cartoons. Some are wood carvings of people and animals. Others are folded paper, such as greeting cards that pop out when unfolded. We've all seen paper and foil Santa Clauses and angels, and of course different kinds of figures made of fired clay. There are even cartoons in wire. Can you recall seeing any of these? In the chapter on sculpture you'll learn about wire figures, and how they are made. They are an excellent example of creative fun.

ALUMINUM COMPANY OF AMERICA

"The Sewing Machine," by Hann Trier.

THE ARTIST

129

A Fun Picture—But Meaningful

Are you surprised to find the picture of a sewing machine in a chapter called "Figures and Faces?" You probably did not know it was a sewing machine until you read the title. Certainly Hann Trier did not paint a realistic sewing machine. Instead he did something much more interesting and amusing.

This sewing machine is going full speed, the wheel is whirring, the needle is chattering, the white thread is jerking, and the action is exciting. Look at the picture and try to imagine that you are stitching as fast as you can make the machine go. What would be your reaction to the machine at such a time?

Hann Trier was really painting a state of mind—the personal feelings of the machine operator. He secured his effect with a clever caricature treatment of the sewing machine.

Make a Cartoon

On page 127 you were asked to make a cartoon. Now that you have done

Two pencil drawings that emphasize action in line. The action should show in the line you draw.

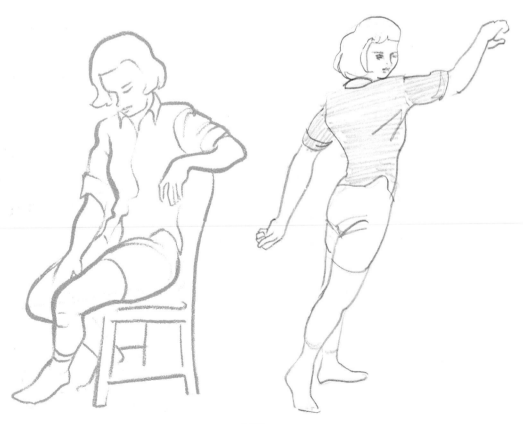

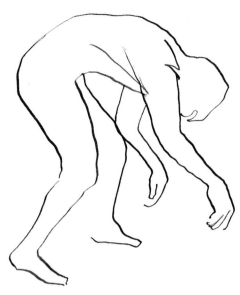

An ink "quickie" of the action lines in a figure. Some of these lines could be eliminated. Which ones are not entirely necessary in depicting the action or position of the figure?

some more studying, try another. Draw it or paint it, or try something different in paper or wire. Let your imagination do the work, and just enjoy experimenting on your own.

Remember some of the important things about cartoons and caricatures. They should emphasize outstanding features. So exaggerate! Make them funny, and if they remind you of something or someone, you'll enjoy them more. Have fun!

EXPERIENCES IN APPRECIATION

1. Try reading character from portrait studies. Select paintings or statues that are known as good character studies.

2. Select a few caricatures of famous people. What makes them look like the real person? A caricature emphasizes certain features.

3. Study fashion drawing for proportions in the figure. Which ones make the clothes look most attractive? Are proportions normal or exaggerated?

4. Make a collection of cartoons. How did the cartoonist tell his story? The stories and subjects are usually based on things that really happened.

CREATIVE ACTIVITIES

1. Make sketches of the human figure standing, sitting, or lying down.

Character portraits emphasize outstanding features, such as the work-worn face of this man.

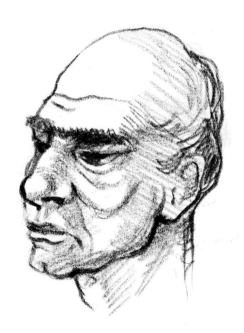

131

Cartoons are often funny drawings of real life.

Select poses which reveal action and movement of line.

2. Make an illustration of something you have done. Use any method you wish. Show several friends in your picture. Your subject might be "At the Football Game," "The Family Watches Television," or "In the Library."

3. Try doing a portrait study of someone you know, or of yourself. Work for a likeness but accent the lines and contours which will portray character.

4. Try to create a figure that is really comic.

5. Try a joke drawing.

6. Cartoon some local happening.

7. Try a painting in a caricature style. (See caricatures on pages 123 and 128.)

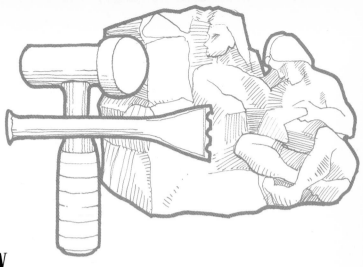

Beauty
in Famous Sculpture

There is a great deal of sculpture in the world. In every land people have modeled in clay and carved from stone and wood. Sometimes they have made tiny statuettes and sometimes colossal figures of amazing size. Sculpture has been created for many reasons, sometimes because of a religious motive, sometimes as a memorial to an important person or for a particular occasion, sometimes to decorate a building, and sometimes for the fun of creating a beautiful effect. Certainly it is not possible for this book to discuss all the statues that were ever important. But a beginning can be made by getting acquainted with a few well known pieces of sculpture which many people have learned to enjoy. Some of these were made centuries ago and have long been famous. Others were created in modern times.

This study is not concerned so much with *when* a statue was made as with *why* it was made, what is its *meaning*, and how to see its *beauty*.

Several famous pieces of sculpture are discussed in the following pages. As you read about each piece try to answer these questions:

1. What idea was the sculptor trying to express?

2. How did he manage to express his idea? What is the appeal of the sculpture?

Some Famous
Memorial Sculptures

A famous statue of Abraham Lincoln is that by the American sculptor Daniel Chester French. The statue, picture on page 134, is in the Lincoln Memorial, Washington, D.C. It is tremendously impressive. The great, seated figure seems to look out across our country through time and foresee what the future holds.

Dramatic night view of Daniel Chester French's statue of Abraham Lincoln, located in the Lincoln Memorial, Washington, D. C.

Everyone knows that Lincoln was a great president who was kind and just, a man with far-seeing vision, one who believed in equal rights for all men. He cared more for the welfare and happiness of the American people than for his own personal life. There is a statue by Augustus Saint-Gaudens on this page which shows some of these characteristics. Lincoln stands with his head slightly bowed, his face serious and sad. His clothing is wrinkled and almost untidy. Behind him is the chair that symbolizes the presidency of the United States of America. But it is not the chair which gives the statue its great dignity and majesty. It is the figure itself, tall, gaunt, and powerful, which is so impressive. Lincoln might have looked so when he delivered his great speech at Gettysburg.

Compare the statues of Lincoln by French and Saint-Gaudens. This does not mean that you have to try to say that one is better than the other. You may prefer one but like the other also. Try to put into words the qualities which are most marked in each statue.

Many thousands of people have seen each of these statues. If you happen to be one of them, describe your visit and your impressions.

The Mount Rushmore National Memorial, located in the Black Hills, South Dakota, is a memorial to four of our great presidents. It was created by the American sculptor Gutzon Borglum. Colossal heads of George Washington, Thomas Jefferson, Theodore

"Lincoln," by Augustus Saint-Gaudens. This statue stands at the entrance to Lincoln Park in Chicago.

Roosevelt, and Abraham Lincoln were sculptured in the rock of the mountainside. The picture on this page does not give an impression of their immense size. Each face, from the chin to the top of the head, measures about sixty feet.

The idea for this memorial was conceived by the sculptor and he was finally commissioned by the federal government to do the work. It was a huge engineering job to cut these enormous heads from the face of the mountain, and many years were required to complete it. The smaller photo on the opposite page shows the size of these heads in comparison to a man. This workman is putting the finishing touches to the head of Thomas Jefferson.

History shows that these four presidents gave great leadership to our nation. The impressive memorial carved on the weather beaten rock of Mount Rushmore is a reminder of their wisdom in the troubled times of the past.

Can you quote a line of wisdom from each of the four presidents? If need be, consult your history books.

The memorial sculptures just discussed were erected in honor of persons whose names are well known and respected. Sometimes a memorial sculpture is erected to honor the deeds of people whose names were never famous. A statue called "The Pioneer Woman," page 138, has been erected in Ponca City, Oklahoma, in honor of the pioneer mothers. Women who joined the pioneer movement in the early days of our country were brave and strong. They rode in covered wagons on rough trails; they suffered the hardships of life in the wilderness; they raised their children without the help of doctors, schools, or churches. This was a great achievement. In "The Pioneer Woman" the sculptor, Bryant Baker, has expressed the courage and strength of these women who helped to settle our western states. The mother strides forward, grasping her son by the hand and carrying her Bible and a bundle of treasured possessions in the other arm.

Famous Tomb Sculpture

Since the earliest days of civilization sculpture has been used to decorate tombs. The cemeteries of today contain many sculptured pieces which mark the graves. Some tomb sculptures both of past and present times have become famous because of their beauty and meaning.

Five thousand years ago in Egypt the great pharaoh Khephren (pronounced Kef′-ren) or Khafre (pronounced Kä′-frå) built one of the great pyramids for his tomb. It took thousands of men many years to build this gigantic stone structure. It is as tall at the peak as a 35-story skyscraper, and spreads out over 13 acres of ground. Why did Khephren want such an enormous tomb? Partly to tell the world what a

great and mighty king he was, but more especially because of what the Egyptians at that time believed about life after death.

They believed that when a person died, a spirit separated from the body at the moment of death. This spirit was invisible and was called a Ka (pronounced Kä). For a time the Ka might live in one's own house but one would not know it because a Ka was invisible. It might live for a time in the body of a cat or beetle. No one ever harmed a cat or a beetle, because if he did he might injure the Ka of someone he had known. Finally the Ka was supposed to wander off into some distant place, a Spirit World, and stay for hundreds, thousands, even hundreds of thousands

Mount Rushmore National Memorial, South Dakota, by the famous American sculptor, Gutzon Borglum.

137

"The Pioneer Woman," by Bryant Baker. Located in Ponca City, Okla.

138

of years. But at some time it would return. When it came back it would look for its own tomb and its own body. If the tomb had not been entered by any living being and the body had not been disturbed, then the Ka could re-enter its own body and would live eternally.

Near the pyramid was another building, known as the Valley Temple. It was a vestibule or entrance. From the temple a covered passageway led to the chapel at the base of the pyramid. Khephren had several statues of himself placed in this Valley Temple. Probably he expected them to serve him after he was dead and buried. Perhaps they were also expected to watch for his Ka when it wandered back from the Spirit World. Or they would help the Ka to find its own body so Khephren would live forever! To us these things seem strange. No one now believes that there is a Ka which will re-enter its own body and bring eternal life. However, it is interesting to study the beliefs and customs of the Egyptian people who lived long ago. It explains for us why Khephren's pyramid was so huge and why his statues stood in the Valley Temple.

When Khephren was buried his people took good care of his pyramid and the other buildings. Every day some of them entered the long covered passageway to the chapel, and there left fresh food. They believed that Khephren's Ka might return at any moment, and when it did there must be fresh food

ready for it. But five thousand years is a very long time. After awhile there were other kings and other things to think about. The pyramid and buildings were left alone and neglected. The winds of the desert blew, and the sands shifted. Finally, the chapel, the passageway, and the temple were entirely covered over. As time went on people forgot that there were any buildings at all near the pyramid. Not till modern times did archeologists dig in the sands around the pyramid and find the ruins of the chapel, the passageway, and the temple.

Sand is heavy and, as you may guess, the buildings had caved in. All the statutes but one in the Valley Temple were broken to bits. You can see some broken places in the remaining Khephren statue on page 140. The original of the statue stands in the museum at Cairo today.

Notice that the end of the beard is broken off. Every Egyptian king had to wear a beard because it was a sign of power, strength, and wisdom. It became the custom for the king sometimes to wear a false beard which he put on just as another king might wear a crown. Khephren's beard rather looks as though it were his own, but in some of the Egyptian statues you can see the straps which hold the beard to the headdress. The headdress was made from a piece of very stiff linen cloth, though it looks in the statue as if it were made from some thick, heavy material.

The early Egyptian sculptors never cut out any open places in their statues. You will see that in the Khephren statue there are no open places under the chair, between the legs, or around the linen headdress. The sculpture is left in one solid piece. It has been suggested that perhaps the stone was too hard and their tools too crude to encourage any extra cutting. Probably this was not the reason. More likely they preferred the heavy, massive effect produced by their solid statues. Perhaps they felt that the statues would endure longer if they were made as strong and solid as possible.

Sculpture for Architectural Decoration and Other Purposes

For many centuries sculpture has been used to decorate buildings. From ancient times down to the twentieth century both interiors and exteriors of temples, churches, and public buildings have been ornamented with statues and bas-reliefs. Bas-relief (pronounced bah-relief) is made by cutting away the background on the surface of a stone slab, so the subject stands out. The two bas-relief sculptures on page 141 decorate the exterior of the building of the Buhl Planetarium and Institute of Popular Science in Pittsburgh, Pennsylvania. Sidney Waugh, an American, is the sculptor. In these two sculptures he has achieved an effect of great power and vitality. The slab called "The Heavens" conveys the feeling of a force, dynamic and powerful beyond

The design on the side of Khephren's chair is hieroglyphic writing. Hieroglyphs are a kind of picture writing. In the upper part of the design is the lotus flower which stands for the Upper Kingdom, the section of Egypt around the upper part of the river Nile. In the lower part of the design is the papyrus which stands for the Lower Kingdom, the part of the country around the delta and mouth of the river. The lines from the lotus and from the papyrus are joined together in a knot. This means that the two kingdoms were joined together under the rule of Khephren. He seems to suggest eternity itself. There is no delicacy or liveliness about it. Instead it is powerful, dignified, majestic. Khephren is every bit a king.

all others. In "The Earth" there is also force and power, but more controlled. This suggests the control that man has achieved over the elements of the world. These sculptures are more decorative than realistic, and represent the strength of Heaven and Earth embodied in human form.

Discuss the sculpture used for architectural decoration in your own community.

Sculpture used for architectural decoration in another age is shown on page 142. Here is the doorway of a cathedral built in the thirteenth century in Bordeaux, France. The figure representing Pope Clement V stands in a dominating position before the central column. On either side are the figures of bishops. Just above the doorway is a row of figures at a table, depicting "The Last Supper." In the second row of figures above the doorway is "The Ascension." In the point of the arch, Christ sits on his throne in Heaven with an angel standing on either side. Kneel-

ing angels just fill the remaining end spaces—a good solution to the sculptor's problem of how to fill the space. In the channels of the great, pointed arch, smaller figures of the saints, disciples, and prophets enhance the form of the arch. Notice how every bit of the decoration conforms to the general shape of the doorway. Good decoration always echoes and enhances the structural form.

Sometimes sculpture is created for the purpose of civic decoration. City authorities commission a sculptor to create a work which will beautify a park or other public place. Of course, such a sculpture may also be a memorial to a person or past event, as in the case of the Columbus Memorial in Washington. Another work by the same sculptor, Lorado Taft, is the Great Lakes Fountain in Chicago. This fountain, on page 143 is a feature in the City Beautiful Plan. Unlike the relief sculptures on this page, the fountain figures are realistic.

Two sculpture decorations by Sidney Waugh on the Buhl Planetarium and Institute of Popular Science.

141

A doorway from the Gothic cathedral in Bordeaux, France, having fine sculpture decorations.

142

"The Fountain of the Great Lakes," by Lorado Taft.

143

Sculptor Taft took as his theme the Great Lakes, which are important to Chicago. From your study of geography you probably have learned that Chicago grew to be a great city partly because of its position on Lake Michigan. The uppermost figure in the fountain represents Lake Superior; immediately below is Huron. Michigan, to the left, pours her waters into Huron's basin. From Huron the water falls into Erie's shell, then into Ontario's, and away to the ocean. The fountain is beautifully designed. The forms are graceful yet strong. Each figure is interesting and yet the whole group is unified and pleasing. Can you trace the main movement in the fountain from figure to figure?

What sculptures are there in your community which you think add to the beauty of the city? Why was each piece erected? What idea was the sculptor trying to express? How well do you think he managed it?

How Sculpture Changes

Sculpture, like painting, has undergone periods of change. Changes are preceded by experiments which influence other artists. You have seen examples of classical Greek "ideal" sculpture, majestic Egyptian tomb statues and carvings, clay and wood figures from mysterious civilizations of the past and present, and a number of monumental works by American sculptors. Each of these types of sculpture evolved from an earlier influence, reflecting the changing customs and cultures of the societies that produced them.

Modern Sculpture

In every endeavor a few people are more creative, more daring, or more ambitious than the average. Sculptors, painters, salesmen, engineers—all include a few who create more imaginatively, who are less likely to be satisfied with things as they are. These are the people who initiate change. Some have been called brilliant, others "mavericks." A maverick is someone who refuses to be like others, or do the expected thing.

Modern sculpture, or sculpture in the twentieth century, reflects a move away from the "garden" and realistic styles of the nineteenth century. The leaders in modern sculpture have created styles that in some cases are like modern painting—that is, abstract, geometric in form, and highly imaginative. They are personal creations by the artists, made for the joy of creating them, and expressing the feelings of the sculptor.

Many sculptors were influenced by the cubist and abstract artists. Cubism is recognized by its geometric arrangements of cubes, prisms, and planes in precise and sometimes intricate designs. It is an abstract form of art, freely departing from realism. The Cubists and Abstractionists found a new way to represent reality. They abstracted or removed unessentials from an idea or subject, then combined the remaining, essential elements with generous portions of pure design. The results were colorful, imaginative, but often mechanical.

The sculpture on this page is called "Man with a Guitar." This cubist figure by Jacques Lipchitz is recognizable as a guitar player, but only the essentials of a real person remain. The artist saw the guitarist as an interesting combination of connecting planes and lines. Unlike some statues in cubist and other styles, this figure appears static. That is, it gives no feeling of motion, each plane or section balancing another.

"The Horse," by Raymond Duchamp-Villon, is another cubist sculpture—perhaps the best ever done. This figure is not static, but suggests strong movement in every part. While at first the horse is not recognizable, another look shows us a single hoof representing all the hooves! With legs together, head down, and back curved, this horse is about to leap like a wild mustang. The coils of the body and strong legs suggest great power. See page 146.

Both of the sculptures above retained the essential shapes of the subjects. The figure by Julio Gonzalez, "Woman Combing Her Hair," is farther from reality. But there are certain shapes and parts that let you see what the artist saw. Can you find them? The

"Man with a Guitar," by Jacques Lipchitz.

145

"The Horse," by Duchamp-Villon.

146

thin, slightly curved rods may represent the hair. The curved metal piece with the elbow-like angle at the bottom suggests the woman's arm above her head. The reverse curve below the arm reminds us of the small of the back. The artist did not intend for us to see arms and hands and head. He shows us the sweep of the back, the bold line of the posture, the movement represented by a woman combing her hair.

When you studied the Greek statue "The Discus Thrower" on page 111, you followed the strong lines and movements of the body. Can you visualize "The Discus Thrower" made in abstract style? How would it look?

Antoine Pevsner, whose sculpture you see on page 148, was interested in space—not outer space, but space that became part of a design. He said that depth alone expresses space. His "Developable Column" illustrates what he said. His metal sculpture, with its beautifully shaped curved planes, reaches into space and returns, measuring it in variable quantities.

Perhaps the best example of a purist in the abstract style is Constantin Brancusi. His work is characterized by its perfection of form. Every sculpture is beautifully modeled, simple in form, and demonstrates a remarkable mastery of the materials from which it is created. See page 149.

"Woman Combing Her Hair," by Julio Gonzalez.

"Developable Column," by Antoine Pevsner.

148

"Bird in Space" is one of many bird forms by Brancusi. The shape of the figure is graceful and subtly curved. It appears to be poised effortlessly, reaching skyward. "Bird in Space" is an idea in solid form.

The elongated shape and decorative quality of the stone head on page 150 reflects the influence of African masks and sculpture. Amedeo Modigliani carved the piece, simply called "Head," to be used as part of a doorway. Its shape is well suited to architectural use, with its vertical emphasis and decorative quality.

The sculptural style of Modigliani is Futurism, although his work shows little of the dream-world qualities that often distinguish this style.

The African mask on page 150 is typical of the carved masks from that great continent. Like other primitive forms of art, it is an honest expression by the artist. Compare this mask with Modigliani's stone head. The mask shows none of the carefully planned proportions evident in the head. Repeated lines in the brow and eyelids and along the side of the head add a decorative pattern to the sculpture. The mask has no brow at all. The sculptor who carved it probably saw the eyes and nose as the important parts of the face. Decoration is an important part of the mask, just as face decoration is important in tribal ceremony.

Compare the two sculptures again and make other comparisons. One is primitive. The other is not. Why?

COLLECTION, THE MUSEUM OF
MODERN ART, NEW YORK

"Bird in Space," by Constantin Brancusi.

African Negro wooden mask.

"Head," by Amedeo Modigliani.

A Personal Touch

A number of artists who looked at abstract sculpture didn't like what they saw. They said it lacked the personal touch, and that a work of art should tell something of the artist's personality. These sculptors turned away from the trend to abstractionism and adopted a personal style. Some of their sculptures were close to reality; others were not. But all show a sense of realism as interpreted by the individual sculptor.

The figure leaning so casually on the little tree is called "Man in the Open Air." It is the work of Elie Nadelman, a sculptor who felt that people pay too much attention to fashion and society. His sculpture is a good-natured joke on the man who concerns himself with trivialities. He tells his joke well, showing us that this fellow's status is measured by his hat and string tie. The statue shows a proud man, one who cuts a smooth figure. Do you agree with this description?

Two other sculptors who have developed personal styles, notable for their honesty, are William Zorach, an American, and Henry Moore, who is British. In his "Head of Christ," Zorach displays his remarkable talent for taking fullest advantage of the material from which he creates his figures. In this head he has combined a feeling of sincerity and simplicity with the structural beauty of black stone. The contrasting textures of the surface

"Man in the Open Air," by Elie Nadelman.

"Head of Christ," by William Zorach.

"Family Group," by Henry Moore.

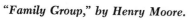

make this figure more vital, more believable. This is a truly beautiful sculpture.

"Family Group" by Henry Moore, opposite, not only represents reality but also suggests the significant ideas underlying the subject. The artist uses rounded shapes to portray the human form and also to give his work vitality. The sense of life can be found in the continuous moving lines that weave themselves among the three figures.

Another sculpture by Henry Moore is "Reclining Figure." Cast in lead, this figure of a woman measures 13 inches long. Like "Family Group," its rounded forms and continuous movement appear to give it life. The figure is abstract in form, emphasizing the essential parts of the body. The arms suggest flexibility and softness, unlike that of a man. The legs are treated as a single form, showing the knees and crossed feet as important parts of the figure. Looking at this figure, you might

think that Mr. Moore is not very complimentary, since this girl appears to have bony knees and very large feet! But truth, not flattery, is the artist's goal, and it is certainly true that not everyone has beautifully shaped limbs.

Look at the illustration on page 154. This sculpture by Alberto Giacometti is called "Chariot." It too may be called abstract, but unlike the other sculptures discussed, it emphasizes only the linear qualities of the subject, and ignores solids or masses. You can see at once that the sculptor considered the wheels of the chariot the essential forms. The man is insignificant, suggesting his relative weakness or unimportance in comparison with the chariot and the powerful horses that pull it.

A number of sculptors today are experimenting with thin metal pieces, including wire, small diameter rods, and metal plates. Wire sculpture is popular as an easy method of expressing form. You'll see a number of examples of

"Reclining Figure," by Henry Moore.

Collection, The Museum of Modern Art, New York

"Chariot," by Alberto Giacometti.

student sculpture at the end of this chapter, along with suggestions for you.

Constructions in Space

In recent years an increasing number of artists have turned to constructions. They use wood, wire, paper, metals, and other materials to create designs in three dimensions. These differ significantly from solid sculptures of stone or metal. Instead of solid forms, they depend upon space or open spaces to create the desired effects. You may recognize the terms *stabile* and *mobile*. Stabiles are secured to a base or other surface. Mobiles are free to move in space, limited only by supporting wires from which the parts are suspended.

Probably the most inventive and widely known mobile sculptor is Alexander Calder. His mobiles may be found in homes, public buildings and private displays across the nation. "Lobster Trap and Fish Tail" hangs from the stairwell ceiling at the Museum of Modern Art in New York City. As you may suppose, the subject or name of the sculpture just gives you a hint about the real meaning of the construction. Mr. Calder once said that his work is really about the universe. His use of detached bodies floating freely in space expresses this idea. Whether or not you visualize bodies in space when you view a Calder mobile, you are fascinated by the beauty of constantly changing and interesting shadow patterns.

Sculpture by Young Americans

In this chapter on sculpture, and in Chapter Nine, Fine Paintings to Remember, you'll have an opportunity to examine works of art by boys and girls your age, who may someday be famous artists. Perhaps you do not draw, paint, or make sculptures yourself; still you should find special pleasure in the young approach to creative art. All of the examples show the freshness of spirit and experimental quality that in

"Lobster Trap and Fish Tail," by Alexander Calder.

the past have led to significant changes in popular forms of art expression.

In recent years art courses in many of our schools have encouraged imagination and individual experimentation. The art class is truly a place where one can find real satisfaction in self-expression. It's not necessary to have special equipment or materials, but

only the desire to interpret honestly one's feelings about an idea or an experience.

Rules of art can sometimes limit your freedom, so when setting out to express yourself, be guided first by the way you feel. Then, if you need help, your teacher can suggest certain principles which you may decide to follow.

When used in this way the formal rules of art do not hinder you, but rather they help you to find the best way of expressing yourself. Of course, your teacher may set limits of size or material, or suggest subject areas, as may be necessary for efficient class operation, but you can be sure the teacher's concern is for the development of your own initiative and creative expression. And certainly nothing should prevent you from experimenting on your own at home.

All examples of student art in this text are by junior and senior high school pupils in the Pittsburgh Public Schools.

Sculptures in Clay

Nearly everyone has made clay sculptures, either in a school art class or at home. Clay has always been a favorite material of sculptors because it can be shaped quickly, changed easily, and lends itself to infinite shapes and surface textures or decoration. Clay is the base from which sculptors cast their metal pieces. Also, those who carve stone usually make clay "sketches" before cutting the final piece, just as a painter often sketches ideas before beginning his canvas.

The three sculptures which follow were made with clay. Each one uses the material in a different way, demonstrating imaginative uses for this material as well as its adaptability to a variety of techniques.

The first is a design in relief on a slab of clay. The young artist, an eighth grader, used a knife, some small pieces of wood, and other "tools" at hand to create this handsome design. It is made up of simple geometric forms that intersect and connect to produce a pattern that reminds us of the cubist sculpture on page 145. The raised parts of the design cast shadows which add variety as the source of light changes. A final surface texture was added by pushing ground, fired clay, called *grog*, into the surface. This sculpture would be used as a wall decoration and should be lighted from above or from the side.

An animal like those in the next illustration might be called a rhinotamus! This is no real animal, of course, but an impression of large animals like the hippopotamus and the rhinoceros. It's an amusing and imaginative sculpture by a tenth grade student. The circles of clay on the backs of the mother and her baby are for decoration only. They're not hair or armor plate—just fun! But they add interest to the figures, creating a texture and pattern different from the smoothness of the bodies. Look again at the differences in texture in Zorach's "Head of Christ," on page 152.

The solid, massive bodies are typical of sculptures in clay. If any thin parts protruded, they might easily be broken off.

The third example is an abstract form. Unlike the animal sculpture, it is

156

SECTION ON ART, PITTSBURGH PUBLIC SCHOOLS

157

158

not recognizable as a real object. Study again for a moment Pevsner's sculpture, "Developable Column." Both Pevsner and the high school student whose sculpture you see on page 158 were interested in space. Space means depth, and both sculptors used thin forms that curve around and partly enclose air spaces. In the student sculpture, the spaces are an important part of the design. They appear to weave through and around the curved forms. This sculpture may be viewed from any angle, the design changing as the form is turned. One might describe the work as a live form, suggesting continuous slow growth. The barklike surface with its incised (cut in) black lines is an interesting contrast to the smooth, jet black interior. The choice of a different color and texture for the inside surface helps to define the shapes more sharply than if both surfaces were identical. This contrast helps to make the sculpture the handsome piece that it is.

Sculptures in Wood

A small handsaw, a coarse file, and sandpaper were the basic tools used to make the two birds. An eleventh grade boy cut them from a piece of mahogany, shaped them with the file, then sanded them smooth. The dowel legs were glued into drilled holes.

The birds are not realistic. Instead, they are the shapes of birds as the artist saw them—smooth, graceful forms that capture the feeling of delicate bodies, capable of swift flight. The elimination of unnecessary details helped achieve this result.

159

TOOLS AND USEFUL SUGGESTIONS FOR WORKING WITH WOOD

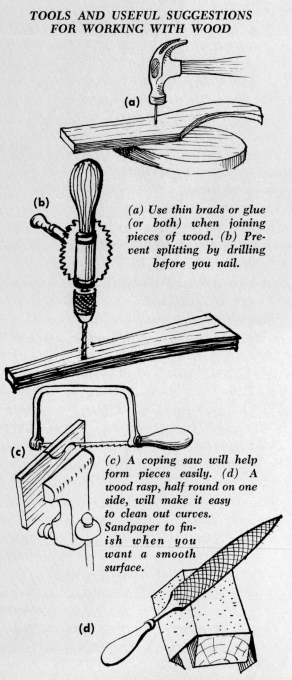

(a)

(b)

(a) Use thin brads or glue (or both) when joining pieces of wood. (b) Prevent splitting by drilling before you nail.

(c)

(c) A coping saw will help form pieces easily. (d) A wood rasp, half round on one side, will make it easy to clean out curves. Sandpaper to finish when you want a smooth surface.

(d)

A natural finish with linseed oil will protect the surface and accent the appearance of the wood grain. This is an excellent finish for hardwoods.

Anyone who has carved wood knows that pieces can easily be split or broken off. The sculptor knew this too, and designed his birds to suit the material. Wood looks more natural when it's smoothly finished in simple shapes. When working with any material, always keep in mind its limitations. Metal pieces can be thin or sharp. They can be bent into angles, curved, or twisted. Wood, however, must be worked in a different way. Each material has its own characteristics. You should be aware of these as you study sculptures, or make them yourself.

The businesslike object you see on page 161 is another abstract. Of course it is not a machine at all, but it does look like one, or several, built to do a hundred jobs.

This design was constructed of scraps from the wood shop. The pieces were selected at random and tacked together to create this amusing structure. You can almost hear it clank and hum! You may want to try a design in wood scraps, or you might choose metal pieces or wire, or perhaps plastic.

Sculptures in Metal

The design, page 162, in black metal and pieces of colored glass is remarkable for its pleasing colors, proportions, and imaginative use of materials. Like the sculpture on page 148, it lets you see through and around its intersecting planes. The scraps of colored glass, one behind the other, permit

light to pass through, creating fascinating color patterns from every angle. This design demonstrates how metal can be cut and bent into delicate, yet strong, supporting members. Could this design be made with wood? In what other ways might the glass pieces be used?

In Chapter Seven, Figures and Faces, you learned about caricatures. Remember that they should look like someone. Caricatures exaggerate outstanding features and make them quickly recognizable.

Animals may be made in caricature too, and they often are. But the one on page 164 is no ordinary caricature, because it's made of wire. The long, large head and sway back make this a very amusing donkey. The orange eye and yellow tail add to the fun.

This lively fellow was literally bent into shape with just a few strands of soft iron wire. A pair of pliers and tacks to hold him upright on the base are all the tools you need—except for your own imagination. Can you think of an animal you could "draw" in wire? At the end of the chapter are some suggestions for getting started.

The two rock-and-roll singers—or should they be called swingers?—were made of wire and pieces of colored metal. Wire was a good choice for these subjects because it's flexible and can be bent freely to any shape. Some wire figures vibrate and sway at a touch— just as you'd expect the guitar playing singers to do.

163

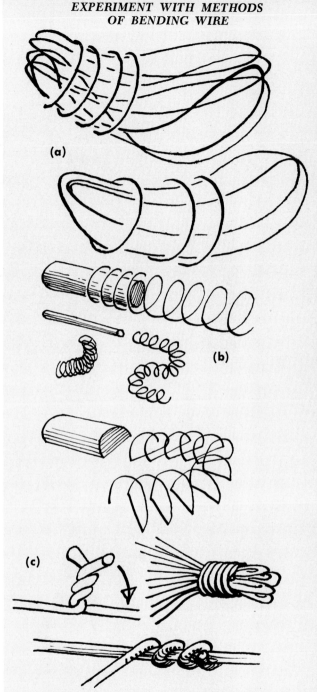

(a) Interesting shapes may be made with many loops of wire—or only a few. (b) Look for forms to use in bending. There are many in your schoolroom or home. Cans, bottles, pieces of wood, and even balls are usable. (c) Attach wires securely! Pliers are a must. Above all, use your imagination!

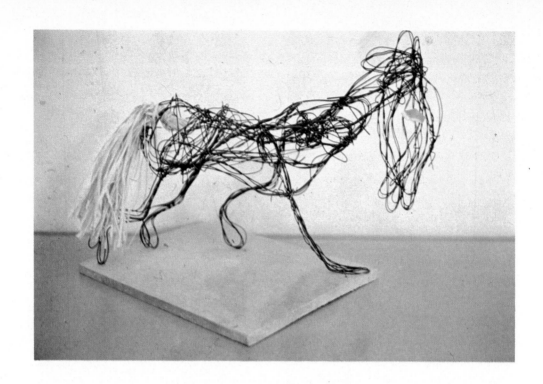

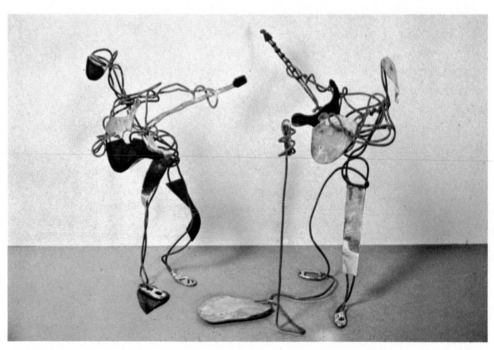

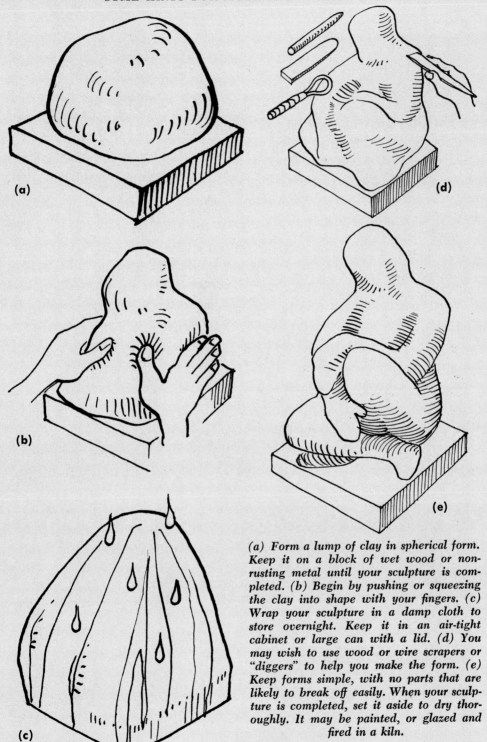

(a) Form a lump of clay in spherical form. Keep it on a block of wet wood or non-rusting metal until your sculpture is completed. (b) Begin by pushing or squeezing the clay into shape with your fingers. (c) Wrap your sculpture in a damp cloth to store overnight. Keep it in an air-tight cabinet or large can with a lid. (d) You may wish to use wood or wire scrapers or "diggers" to help you make the form. (e) Keep forms simple, with no parts that are likely to break off easily. When your sculpture is completed, set it aside to dry thoroughly. It may be painted, or glazed and fired in a kiln.

165

Sculpture in our Homes

We have been discussing famous sculptures located in parks, art galleries, and other places. Certainly we can enjoy them in their settings, or find pleasure in looking at pictures of them. But we can enjoy sculptures every day if we have them in our homes. There are many fine carvings and figures of people and animals for use in smaller areas. There are places in your home where one of these would fit in just right. Or you may wish to make your own, as other students have done. In the section on CREATIVE ACTIVITIES you'll learn more about how to create sculptures for yourself.

EXPERIENCES IN APPRECIATION

1. Become acquainted with several famous sculptures not shown in this book. Be prepared to discuss them. Report on the person or event to which the sculptures were erected. Explain how the sculptor expressed his idea and show how well he did it.

2. Select some past event in your own community which you think is worthy of a memorial sculpture. Try to create in your mind an idea for this memorial. This does not require ability to do sculpture, but thinking and imagination.

3. What is your favorite piece of sculpture? Why?

4. Select a theme such as Indian sculpture. Collect information and pictures about your subject. Report to the class. Other themes which you might choose are Sculpture for Our Homes, Animal Sculpture, or Gods and Goddesses in Sculpture.

5. Most great sculptures are created first by means of clay modeling. Then the model is translated into stone or bronze. If possible arrange for a demonstration of molding from a clay model.

6. Survey your community with the idea that a statue can be erected for beautification. What do you think it should be? Where should it be placed?

7. Arrange a demonstration, perhaps for an auditorium program, by a local sculptor.

CREATIVE ACTIVITIES

1. Choose a subject which interests you for clay modeling. It should be something with which you are familiar, such as your pet dog or cat, your favorite animal in the zoo, a horse, or head. You might want to do a caricature in clay.

Before you begin modeling, think of the special characteristic which you wish to emphasize most. The figure should be at least 6 inches high.

When the model is partly completed, hold a class consultation on the success of the work. Be prepared to give suggestions to others and to receive them yourself. Remember that your piece should emphasize the characteristic which you selected. Continue to work for the best expression of it which you can make.

2. Choose a subject for a bas-relief in clay modeling. It might tell a story, or be a design such as you saw on page 157.

Keep the composition of the bas-relief simple. It should be at least 8 inches by 12 inches.

3. Make a simple sculpture in wood. Remember that wood splits easily, so choose a shape that will not be hard to form. Look at the birds on page 159.

4. Arrange wood scraps, metal pieces, tile, or other odds and ends in a design. The pieces may be glued or nailed, or pushed into wet plaster.

5. Make some wire figures or animals. Practice bending and working the wire before you begin on your first figure. You may use wire from 18 to 22 gauge. Gauge 18 is heavier than 22.

6. Try some caricatures in wire. Exaggerate!

Fine Paintings to Remember

Most of us cannot afford to buy all the fine pictures that we would like to own. However, the lack of money need not prevent us from becoming acquainted with a few of the world's great paintings. We can learn to know and enjoy them, even though we cannot own them. Anyone can stand before a beautiful picture in an art gallery and enjoy it just as much as the man who can write a check and take it home with him. Of course, the man who has a private art gallery can look at his pictures often and enjoy their beauty, but the rest of us can enjoy our memories of the fine pictures that we have seen. Our own private art galleries are in our heads. They can bring us a great deal of satisfaction and pleasure. These mental picture galleries cost us nothing but the time spent in getting acquainted with the pictures.

A study of great paintings can be a lifetime work. For hundreds of years, artists have been painting fine pictures. Our private picture galleries can hold only a few of these thousands of paintings. A relatively few paintings have been selected for you to add to your private "collection" in this chapter. They have not been chosen because they are the most famous, or the most valuable, or the most beautiful, but because they are favorites with a great many boys and girls and therefore a part of the beauty to be found in their world.

Three Landscapes—
All Different

There are many things to see in the great outdoors—trees, hills, mountains, valleys, clouds, rivers, and lakes. From all this, the landscape painter must choose the things that will go into his picture. He must decide also what

"The Bridge of Trysts," by Corot.

effect or impression he wants in his painting. He may wish to have a pretty, peaceful little scene or perhaps a mighty and exciting effect. There are many different kinds of landscapes, and we can enjoy each one for what it shows us.

The landscape pictured on this page can be found in France. It was painted by Jean-Baptiste Camille Corot (Kō-rō´). Corot was born in 1796 and died in 1875. He painted landscapes with poetic effects. In this one we see talking and waiting figures at a place where lovers were said to meet. The figures, however, are not the most important part of the picture. The soft mass of foliage arched in the sky beyond the bridge and the slender, graceful tree trunks at the left are what give the painting its delicate and poetic effect.

Corot spent a great deal of time outdoors with his sketchbook. He tramped the woods and the fields studying trees, skies, clouds, and streams. Many of his trips were early in the morning because he especially liked the misty twilight effects which come just before the

"Stone City, Iowa," by Grant Wood.

daybreak. Because he carried sketchbook and pencils with him, he was considered a little peculiar. One hundred years ago in France, artists did all their work in their studios. It was most unusual for an artist to do any drawing or painting outdoors where he could see the actual scene. In fact, landscapes themselves were practically unknown in French art until the time of Corot. They had been used chiefly as backgrounds or settings for pictures with people as the chief interest. Portraits, religious themes and Greek myths were subjects for paintings. Landscape alone had not been considered a worthy subject for a picture. Artists of other countries had painted landscapes, but French artists up until this time had not wanted to devote their time to it. You can see why Corot was considered strange and why his work was not popular at the time. He did not sell a picture until he was nearly fifty years old. People didn't want his pictures. However, he could spend his time at painting instead of earning a living because his father gave him a small allowance. When Corot was young his father had hoped he would go into the linen business with him, but Corot wanted to paint. Finally his father allowed him to go to Italy and study. In later years Corot moved from Paris to the village of Barbizon, located near Fontainebleau Forest. There he discovered the beauty of nature and put it into his paintings.

Several other artists, friends of Corot's, also lived at Barbizon and painted outdoors. This group of artists is known as the Barbizon School.

In the later years of Corot's life his work became very popular and he sold a great many pictures at high price. The public had decided that, after all, landscapes could make beautiful pictures.

"Stone City, Iowa," by Grant Wood

Grant Wood, a famous American artist, was known as a "regional painter," which means that he chose to paint pictures of people and places in his own part of the country—Iowa. He once studied in Paris, France, sometimes called the art center of the world. After a time, he said he thought there was plenty to paint in Iowa, so he went back home and remained there the rest of his life, painting pictures of people and things with which he was familiar. John Steuart Curry, who painted "The Tornado" (page 177) was another regional artist, painting life in Kansas.

In the painting on page 170, Grant

"America," by Rockwell Kent.

THE ARTIST

171

"End of Day," by Charles Burchfield.

Wood chose as his subject a small town in his home state. He shows us a view of the town such as we might see from an airplane flying at low altitude. Grant Wood painted in his own individual way. Unlike Corot, Grant Wood made his picture into a kind of design or pattern. The cornfield is an allover decorative pattern; the trees are like models; the houses appear as little boxes; and the hills are modeled as in a scene on a sand table. It is Grant Wood's way of portraying a scene in Iowa. We cannot help but like his way of showing us beauty in our country. The solid forms and the feeling of great distance are recognizable features of Grant Wood's paintings.

"America," by Rockwell Kent

Here is another modern landscape, page 171, but one that is painted in an entirely different manner. Its name gives us a clue to its meaning. It symbolizes our great country and the pioneers who settled it. There is a wooded hilltop in the foreground, a vast expanse of plains beyond, and in the distance great mountains. The sun spotlights the scene with a clear, strong light. The little log cabin in the near foreground stands for all the log cabins built by brave pioneers. Near it a man chops wood, symbolizing what man has done in the struggle to settle this country, and on the other side of the cabin a woman hangs laundry on the line, symbolizing woman's share of work in the pioneer movement. The artist has expressed these ideas in his own style. He gives us a feeling of vast spaces, majestic heights, and never-ending skies.

Rockwell Kent also is a twentieth-century American artist. He traveled and painted in Alaska, Greenland, and other out-of-the-way places. On his travels he found ideas for his landscapes.

Towns and Cities—Two Pictures

There was a time when painters thought that a beautiful outdoors scene could be found only in the country. Then some of them found that there is beauty in buildings and bridges, city streets, factories, and village houses.

"End of Day,"
by Charles Burchfield

Would you think of looking for a beautiful picture in a village street of dingy houses? The American artist Charles Burchfield found one on a winter day in a mining town. He called it "End of Day." See page 172. Men are coming home from their work, and daylight has begun to fade. The houses are old and ramshackled, but Burchfield has painted them as he might paint people—with personalities of their own. Notice that as you look into the picture you look down the street. It is a fine piece of perspective drawing. Perhaps you will say, "This is not a pretty picture." Perhaps it is not pretty, but it has a kind of honest beauty. Burchfield's subjects are common, everyday scenes, and often they are not pretty. But the way they are painted makes them seem picturesque and

"Steel, Steam, and Smoke," by Everett Warner.

sometimes romantic. Corot made his landscapes romantic, and in a way Burchfield does the same thing with his ugly village street. He is a poet in paint.

"Steel, Steam, and Smoke," by Everett Warner

Some artists find beauty in the busy turmoil of a great industrial city. Everett Warner has shown us beauty in a view of Pittsburgh's steel mills. See page 173. In the foreground we see a small house and yard surrounded by a dilapidated fence. Across the river there are giant smokestacks which belch forth great clouds of smoke and steam. The plain little house is the center of interest; it is interesting to see how Warner managed to emphasize it. Not only is it near the center of the canvas but its light color stands out against a darker background. The fence and roadway help to set it apart from the remainder of the scene. Altogether, the artist has created a picture with interesting composition. The lines and forms are put together well. You will be interested to know that Warner painted the scene as it really is and changed nothing. He searched the city until he found a spot where he could paint a picture as the scene really was, and at the same time have a pleasing composition. Of course, he emphasized certain things and subordinated others. He did not show every detail of the houses at the edges of the picture, nor did he make them stand out so distinctly as the house in the center. Although this picture is a truthful representation of the scene, it could never be mistaken for a photograph.

Select a scene in your community which is generally thought of as lacking beauty. Can you see it as Everett Warner might have painted it? Even if you cannot paint it to your own satisfaction, you can explain how you would plan the picture.

Portraits in Paint

Pictures of people have been popular subjects for painting since its beginning. Some artists like to paint portraits so much that they confine themselves entirely to that kind of painting.

You have already looked at two portraits. Remember "The Laughing Cavalier" and the Japanese gentleman in Chapter Seven? These were both men-about-town. Their clothing and expressions showed this.

Two Self-Portraits by Rembrandt

Sometimes artists paint pictures of themselves. On page 175 you will see two portraits of the same man, both painted by himself. What can you read from these portraits about the man himself? Of course, you will see at once that in one portrait he is young and in the other he is old. What more can you discover in the faces?

Discuss what you see in these portraits. How did Rembrandt feel about himself and his life in each case? After you have done your best, read the following story.

174

Two self-portraits by Rembrandt.

Rembrandt Harmenszoon van Rijn lived three hundred years ago in Holland. His long name means that he was Rembrandt, son of Harmens, of the Rhine. His father was a miller whose mill stood on the Rhine River. By the time Rembrandt was fifteen his father saw that his son was not much good at anything except art, so Rembrandt was apprenticed to an artist. As a young man Rembrandt moved to Amsterdam and soon became the leading artist in the city. His pictures were popular.

He married a beautiful girl named Saskia. He adored his Saskia, and dressed her in silks and velvets and adorned her with jewels. Naturally he painted many portraits of Saskia. He, too, liked to dress in expensive clothing and show himself as a fine gentleman. He also bought many paintings and other works of art until his house became a museum. He and Saskia lived in a grand manner and spent a great deal of money. In spite of his many commissions and high prices, he spent more than he made. The first portrait of himself was painted during this period of his life when he was popular and famous. You can see his fine clothes. You can see, too, that he was proud and perhaps a little vain. He was full of self-confidence and a trifle boastful.

Up to this time Rembrandt's life was a success story. Then, when he was thirty-six years old, two catastrophes befell him: Saskia died; the public turned against his pictures.

It was the fashion in Rembrandt's time for groups of men such as the officers of a militia company or the heads of a business organization to commission a painter to do a group portrait of themselves. The officers of Captain Banning Cock's civic guards ordered a group portrait from Rembrandt. They expected to see themselves standing or sitting in a group around a table, each in an equally prominent position. Rembrandt painted a huge canvas showing the company as it sallied forth at noon on its way to do guard duty on the city walls. Naturally the first figures were in full sunlight, but others were caught in the shadow of the great gateway. The faces of a few men show clearly, but others are hidden by those in front and obscured by shadow. This did not please the officers at all, especially those in the background. There was a great row about it. Rembrandt refused to change it because he knew it was a good picture and that it would be ruined if every face and figure were equally prominent.

The picture was called "The Sortie of the Banning Cock Company." Sortie means a sudden charge into the open by a group of soldiers. The company would not hang the picture in the great room for which it was intended and instead put it into a small anteroom. In order to make it fit the wall space they cut off a strip at one side, spoiling the balance and composition. Later it was hung in a room which was heated with a peat fire. The black smoke from the burning peat covered the picture with a layer of soot. This so darkened the canvas that people came to believe it was meant for a night picture and called it "The Night Watch." That is the name by which it is generally known today. Remember that it was really a picture at high noon with full sunlight! The picture now occupies a room by itself in the museum in Amsterdam.

After the Guard portrait, Rembrandt received very few commissions. His creditors forced him into bankruptcy. His house, his art collections, his own paintings, and even his clothing were sold for debt. He moved to a smaller, poorer house. His struggles with poverty were long and hard. However, he continued to paint. Sometimes he had difficulty in obtaining colors and canvas for his pictures, but he managed. Perhaps for want of other subjects, he continued with self-portraits. The second portrait on page 175 was painted in 1662, a few years before his death. Here is a man who is sad and disillusioned. The world has treated him harshly, but he is patient and philosophical. It is hard to believe that this is the same man as the confident young fellow in the earlier portrait.

Dramatic and Exciting Subjects—Two Pictures

Sometimes artists choose subjects that are dramatic and exciting. Moments of danger and tragedy expressed

"The Tornado," by John Steuart Curry.

in paint can be as exciting as on the stage, screen, or TV. In these two pictures you will see how two American artists have used a tornado and a prize fight as subjects for exciting and dramatic pictures.

"The Tornado," by J. S. Curry

"The Tornado," by John Steuart Curry, shown on this page, tells its own story. A great, swirling funnel rushes over the prairie toward the farm home. The big farmer holding his little girl by the hand, looks back, urging the boys to hurry. The boys are running, one carrying a clawing black cat, the other two little pigs. The mother, holding the baby and wide-eyed with apprehension, is just entering the cyclone cellar. It is all swift, dramatic movement. It catches the fearful moment before the tornado strikes.

Curry grew up on a Kansas farm, and he painted his picture from memories of tornadoes in his boyhood. His favorite subjects for painting were farm animals, storms, and rural scenes from the Middle West, especially Kansas.

"Dempsey and Firpo," by George Bellows

George Bellows, also an American artist, has given us another kind of dramatic picture. His painting "Dempsey and Firpo" shows us a powerfully

177

dramatic moment in a famous prize fight. Jack Dempsey, as you probably know, held the championship for heavyweights. He was challenged by Luis Angel Firpo, a South American of tremendous strength, sometimes called the "Wild Bull of the Pampas." Dempsey won the fight, but during the battle Firpo managed to knock Dempsey through the ropes into the laps of some spectators. Such a thing had never happened before in modern heavyweight boxing. Hence this is the moment that Bellows chose to portray. It is a picture of furious action and terrific excitement.

Bellows was a good athlete himself. In fact he almost became a professional baseball player instead of an artist. He painted other exciting pictures of prize-fights, polo games, and other sports. But he could also paint quiet pictures. Sometime you may become acquainted with his very fine portraits of his mother and his children.

From your study of "Dempsey and Firpo" would you say that Bellows' work is realistic, romantic, or imaginative? Why?

Styles in Painting

The paintings talked about so far in this chapter were chosen for subject matter—landscapes, cities and towns, and portraits. These paintings represented different times and different styles.

Chapter Eight, on sculpture, took up styles in art. You'll recall that style

"Dempsey and Firpo," by George Bellows.

"The Lion Hunt," by Eugene Delacroix.

changes are brought about by the influence that experimenters have on others. This is true of painting when artists look for new or more creative ways to express themselves.

Painting has experienced changes through the centuries, from the time when man first painted or carved pictures on stone to the present day.

A Century of Painting

From 1850 to the present at least eight important styles of painting developed. Six of these represent the most lasting: Romanticism, Impressionism, Post-Impressionism, Cubism, Abstractionism, and Surrealism. They will be discussed here.

Romanticism

In the middle 1800's young painters tired of the severe style that had characterized the early part of the century. Certain artists who then began to paint are known as the Romantic painters, so-called because they revived rich colors, exciting action, and the romance of adventure in foreign lands. Eugene Delacroix's "The Lion Hunt" is an excellent example of Romantic painting, capturing the thrill of the hunt in vivid colors, violent action, and glamorous beauty.

Impressionism

Impressionist French painters, beginning about 1870, experimented with

179

"*On the Terrace,*" *by Pierre Auguste Renoir.*

COLLECTION, THE MUSEUM OF MODERN ART, NEW YORK.
ACQUIRED THROUGH LILLIE P. BLISS BEQUEST

"Starry Night," by Vincent Van Gogh.

paints and colors, attempting to represent the warmth of real sunlight, the shimmering greens and blues of trees and sky, the rich skin tones of women and children. They used small strokes of different colors close together so that when viewed from several feet away the colors blended, and were rich and more iridescent or shining than when painted in broader strokes. Among the masters of Impressionism was Pierre Auguste Renoir, whose painting "On the Terrace" is famous for the depth and realism of its colors. The Impressionists were also realists, as the painting shows. Their subjects were people and places that they knew well.

Post-Impressionism

Post-Impressionism found popularity near the end of the nineteenth century. The painters who represented this period developed individual styles of their own. They left realism and broke painting rules to experiment with form, pattern, and color.

In "Starry Night," Vincent Van Gogh describes an ordinary scene in a

181

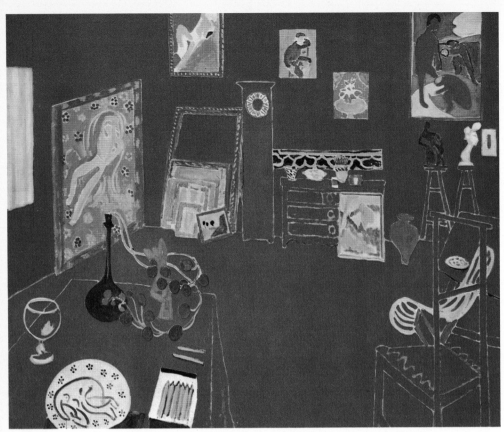

COLLECTION,
THE MUSEUM
OF MODERN ART,
NEW YORK.
MRS. SIMON
GUGGENHEIM
FUND

*"The Red Studio,"
by Henri Matisse.*

most imaginative way. The unnaturally brilliant colors in the stars and moon, and the swirling curves in far-away galaxies, are a sharp departure from the painting style of the Impressionists.

At the turn of the century the Paris public was shocked at an exhibit of brilliant colors and unusual design by Post-Impressionists. A newspaper critic described the paintings as barbaric. Another named these painters "Les Fauves," which means the wild beasts.

Les Fauves were the mavericks or rebels among painters. Their paintings were brilliant in color, bold in design, and decorative rather than realistic. Henri Matisse was a leader among these artists, developing a flat, two-dimensional style of his own. His painting "The Red Studio" is as exciting and colorful as the imagination allowed. The painting is not as haphazard as it first appears to be. The alternately bold areas and delicate lines create a pattern that holds together well, while the viewer finds himself "traveling" around the perimeter of the room, examining each interesting item along the way.

Cubism

In the study of sculpture, Chapter Eight, is a figure of a man with a guitar. The rectangular forms and connecting planes identified the sculpture as Cubist. This style developed out of Post-Impressionism.

The Cubist painters found their way of art in systematic and mechanical designs. Their paintings appeared as geometric symbols, repeated and interconnected to produce surprisingly strong and sustained rhythms. The Cubists were abstract rather than realistic. Therefore they developed individual techniques for describing their ideas.

Juan Gris developed a technique of Cubist collage, in which paint, paper, and other materials are combined. In "Breakfast" Gris used wood-grain

"Breakfast," by Juan Gris.

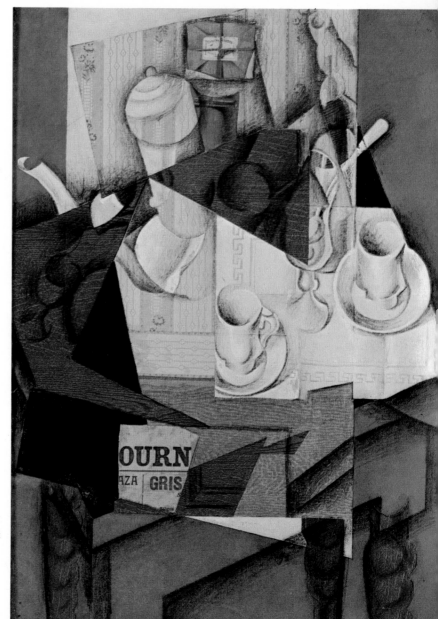

183

paper, a piece of real newspaper, a tobacco pouch stamp on the orange package. Other articles are modeled in relief or painted on the surface. The design is well balanced, carefully planned, and the colors are subdued. The rather conservative coloring serves to emphasize the shapes and pattern in the design. Many experiments have been made in Cubist collage.

Abstractionism

As just noted, the Cubists were Abstractionists. An abstract work of art has been described as one that combines the essentials of an idea with elements of pure design.

Pablo Picasso is probably the most popular and prolific painter of this century. He has experimented with a variety of styles, but he is most famous for his Cubist and abstract painting.

In 1920 Picasso was commissioned to design costumes for a ballet, "Pulcinella." This task led to his painting "Three Musicians." These were characters from the play upon which the ballet was based. Pierrot plays the recorder, Harlequin strums the guitar, while the bearded monk sings to their

"The Three Musicians," by Pablo Picasso

*"Improvisation
No. 30,"
by Wassily
Kandinsky.*

accompaniment. This is one of Picasso's best. Gay figures combined with beautiful patterns make this a fine abstract. But it was Picasso who said, "People who try to explain pictures are usually barking up the wrong tree." No more about the musicians!

The most influential Abstractionist was Wassily Kandinsky, who went from Les Fauves painting to abstract and non-objective. Non-objective means that it does not represent a real object. Look at Kandinsky's painting on this page, "Improvisation No. 30." The artist was not interested in a realistic picture, but preferred to create effects which would appeal to the imagination or emotions. The splashes of bright colors and sharp lines might suggest the sights and sounds of a city—a noisy city! What else could this painting represent?

Surrealism

The Surrealists explored a world of hallucination or unreality. Their paintings suggest mysterious places where anything can happen—and does. Eerie

"Composition,"
by Joan Miro.

landscapes and unreal shapes are painted in startling detail, almost as if they did exist; sometimes they are portrayed in shadow forms that suggest strange animals and unfamiliar beings.

Most Surrealists created paintings that appeared to be actual scenes of dream worlds. Others, like Joan Miro, produced less fantastic, but just as imaginative, canvases. Miro's "Composition" is a scene of unusual, ghostlike figures suspended in a strange atmosphere. Some of the shapes suggest animal forms, while others could be trees or growths from another world. It may be that we are looking at ghost animals, some with long horns, while

nearby a dog contemplates in amazement what he sees before him. Unlike the more fantastic Surrealist paintings, this one is beautiful for its color and composition, yet it retains mysterious qualities. What do you see in Miro's painting?

Miro's painting can also be identified as belonging to another style, besides Surrealism. Of the styles already discussed, which would it fit?

Primitive Painters

Primitive painting and sculpture cannot be classified chronologically as a major period in art, but primitive has always been one of the most significant forms of expression. Its beginning paralleled the development of early man, even before the time of the cave paintings of Altamira (page 31). There will probably be primitive painters as long as men live on earth.

Primitive may be defined as untrained or, as one primitive painter describes himself, self-taught. Primitive painters and sculptors do not follow mechanical rules or methods such as perspective and proportion. Their works are spontaneous and original, simple expressions of their minds'-eye view of the subject. The African mask on page 150 is an example of primitive sculpture.

The paintings below and on page 188 are fine examples of this style.

They are simple and beautiful impressions of experiences from the lives of the painters.

The first, "And the Migrants Kept Coming," was painted by Jacob Lawrence. It is part of a series called the Migration of the Negro, a collection of sixty panels depicting the life of the Negro. Half of this collection is in the Phillips Gallery in Washington, D.C. The other thirty panels are exhibited at the Museum of Modern Art in New York City.

The figures crowded together on the railroad station platform are woven into a design of light and dark patches so that they almost lose their identity. This group of people must have appeared to the painter as a living pattern

"And the Migrants Kept Coming," by Jacob Lawrence. **187**

COLLECTION, THE MUSEUM OF MODERN ART, NEW YORK. GIFT OF MRS. DAVID M. LEVY

"Bushmen Running from the Rain," by J. Ndandarika.

of colors, just as you have seen at a parade or in the bleachers at a ballgame. Details are unimportant except for the part they play in the pattern of shapes and colors. "Barbados Children," on page 122, has some of the same characteristics. Can you explain what that statement means?

The painting above was made by an African, J. Ndandarika. Mr. Ndandarika is the painter who described himself as self-taught. He calls his painting "Bushmen Running from the Rain." The heavy clouds pouring out their deluge of rain, and the men running for shelter, must have been felt very strongly by the artist. Looking at this picture we can almost feel the wetness of the warm rain and the spongy turf underfoot. Have you ever seen a cloudburst painted in a more convincing manner? What makes the storm look so real? Remember what you learned about the ability of color to describe a mood, or to make us feel warm or cold. The primitive artist paints what he sees, but he emphasizes what he feels.

Another Way to Paint

On this page is an engraving. Engraving is another way to "paint," although the artist uses a metal plate upon which he carves or etches the lines to reproduce a drawing. You examined woodcuts in Chapter Seven, Figures and Faces. These represent still another way to "paint."

This engraving is called "David in the Wilderness." The artist, Norma Morgan, has made David a tiny mortal figure among the massive rocks and vegetation that grows upon them. It is more forcible in color. In this scene, David has fled to the wilderness to escape King Saul who had threatened to kill him. David had slain Goliath, and the people praised him, saying that Saul had killed his thousands, and David his ten thousands. In a fit of jealous anger, Saul ordered his servants to seek out and kill David. The engraving shows David hiding out.

The engraving is a striking composition of lights and darks, with each rock and patch of vegetation an intricate and beautifully drawn design of its own. One needs to look closely to appreciate fully the richness of decorative forms that make up the engraving pattern.

COLLECTION, THE MUSEUM OF MODERN ART, NEW YORK.
ABBY ALDRICH ROCKEFELLER FUND

*"David in the Wilderness,"
by Norma C. Morgan.*

189

Paintings by Young Americans

In Chapter Eight, Beauty in Famous Sculpture, you studied examples of works by young Americans—students in junior and senior high school art classes. Some were made to represent familiar subjects, either people or animals. A few were abstract or non-objective. Refer to the definitions of these terms on pages 184 and 185.

In early civilizations, man recorded his experiences by carving in stone or painting the walls of caves. These first artists told us most of what we know about man's early history. They chose the most important facts to record—how they provided food for their families, how they dressed and where they lived, who their gods, priests, and chieftains were. No matter which age we study, whether the time of the cave dwellers, the Middle Ages, or the present, our knowledge of our ancestors and even of ourselves is enhanced by the collection of works of art through which man has told his own story. This story has many chapters, some sad and tragic, some happy, some real, others imaginative.

As you studied the previous paintings selected for this chapter you probably were aware that most of them told stories about people. Even those identified as abstract or non-objective tell us something important about man—that he continues to search for new ideas and new ways to express himself. Haven't you often wanted to try something new, to experiment with new ideas?

The seven paintings which follow tell us a story of people your age—through the eyes of young artists. Like paintings by artists from all periods in history, they are based on the personal experiences and feelings of the painters.

A Self-Portrait

In Chapters Seven and Eight you studied a number of portraits. One was

SECTION ON ART, PITTSBURGH PUBLIC SCHOOLS

a self-portrait by Heckel, the woodcut on page 120. On page 175 of this chapter you studied two self-portraits by Rembrandt. All three told stories about the artists.

The self-portrait on page 190 tells a story too. It says that this young artist has identified herself as a student. If you could paint yourself, would you include pencil and books, or would you identify yourself as a skater, water skier, dancer, fisherman, or as a pilot, or would you simply be surrounded by friends? True artists who paint themselves always disclose some intimate details of their personalities.

Two Pictures of Friends

Paintings of friends have always been popular subjects with artists. Friends are important to all of us, but especially to young people who may measure happiness by their social standing, or by the number of friends they have.

The first picture, a painting, tells a story of a girl who is well-liked even by younger girls. Some people have friends only in their own age group. Others enjoy associating with all ages. In this painting it's easy to see that the younger girls look up to the oldest of the group because she willingly and patiently answers the many questions they have. This is a real situation, one that you might have experienced, too. Which girl in the picture would you identify with yourself? What other story can you read in this painting?

SECTION ON ART, PITTSBURGH PUBLIC SCHOOLS

A real situation is good for a beginning when you're ready to paint a picture. Can you explain why this is true?

The next picture is an ink drawing; for this reason you may think it does not belong in a chapter on painting. But it's here to tell another story about friends, and about the artist. Compare this drawing with the painting of the girls. How do they differ in the way that the artists treated their subjects? Would you agree that the painting shows more concern about how the girls felt than how they looked? The drawing is just the opposite. The talented young artist who drew this picture saw his subjects as interesting parts of a

191

design—a realistic design to be sure, but decorative and sensitive to the shapes, lines, and textures of the subjects. You have seen other paintings in this book which depicted people as interesting parts of a design. Which ones were they?

You might wish to try some ink drawings yourself. At the end of Chapter Seven, Figures and Faces, are some suggestions for drawing people in ink.

Two Landscapes

Many of the world's most famous painters prefer to paint things as they are, or as they happened. A realistic painting can be dramatic or peaceful or mysterious. Curry's painting of the tornado on page 177 and Bellow's fight scene on page 178 are certainly dramatic. Corot's landscape on page 169,

however, is a peaceful scene. It has a different kind of force.

The painting on page 193 would fit the definition of mysterious. Or you may prefer to call it spooky! This scary old house, standing so quiet and still on a deserted street, is the artist's impression of a real house on a real street. The subdued blues that dominate the painting add a chill to the scene, and suggest that the night will be long, the rain steady and cold. No one would like to venture out on such a night or be alone in such a house! This painting is a good example of how an artist can create a mood. In this case, the mood was created by emphasizing the loneliness of the scene, the wierdness of the house, and by selecting colors that are gray-blue and chilling.

Now picture the same house, in good

repair, on a bright sunny day, with children playing in the street and mother standing on the porch. What a difference these changes would make to the same house on the same street!

The river scene below is a real place, too. The artist has emphasized the wetness of the scene by painting it in water color with a quick, free style. Water color paintings usually have a wet or fluid appearance because the paint flows easily and dries without leaving ridges. Water colorists seldom brush the paint back and forth. They usually wet the paper first, then paint boldly and quickly, allowing the colors to mix by flowing together. Water color can produce beautiful, moving effects.

This painting of the river was made on the spot. Remember that personal knowledge of the subject makes the picture more believable.

SECTION ON ART, PITTSBURGH PUBLIC SCHOOLS

193

SECTION ON ART, PITTSBURGH PUBLIC SCHOOLS

Two Collages

A collage is made by gluing pieces of flat materials to a background. This technique is sometimes combined with painting. You studied a famous example of collage on page 183. It was "Breakfast," by Gris.

The unusual design in yellow, orange, and shades of violet pictured opposite was made of pieces of tinted transparent material, cellophane or other soft plastic. It was cut, folded, and wrinkled, then glued to a board. The use of transparent sheets adds a dimension of depth by letting us see through the overlapped pieces. Each layer changes the depth of color. This is an imaginative use of new materials for an experiment.

The second collage might be called a pattern of ideas—a student's ideas about the future. He is confronted with making a choice of his next step in education or training for an occupation. He sees that endless opportunities present themselves to a person who is capable, and willing to learn. This decorative panel would be a useful addition to a school bulletin board. How is it like a poster?

195

colorful design pictured here includes pieces of broken tile and some articles of hardware—nuts and nails. The lively pattern of blues and red-orange is out of the ordinary. It combines interesting surface textures with a bright color on neutrals of different shades. Painters often use this "materials" technique only in small areas of a painting to call attention to a particular part of the composition.

You might wish to try an experiment with a mosaic design. It should be pleasing to the eye, and the colors and materials carefully chosen. It would be very easy to create a hodge-podge of scraps instead of a handsome panel. A mosaic requires as much planning as a painting, but once you have your design laid out, it can be completed in a short time. The section on CREATIVE ACTIVITIES at the end of the chapter includes some hints as guides for making a mosaic.

A Survey of Your Private Picture Gallery

You have learned about different kinds of fine paintings and other pictures in this chapter. You may wish to add others to your private mental gallery. You have studied paintings by famous artists and by some that may become famous. You can refer to them again and again with pleasure, and it is hoped that by learning about them you will look for fine paintings wherever you are.

A Mosaic

The last "painting" in this chapter is also a kind of collage, but it was made of solid materials pushed into wet plaster. This design is a mosaic, a form of creating permanent designs, pictures, and murals that has been in use for many centuries. It is still a popular form of decoration for large areas both inside and outside of buildings. The

Artists usually prefer to paint certain kinds of subjects—portraits, landscapes, dramatic events, or abstract compositions. Those who simply look at paintings have favorites, too. Look over the paintings again and decide which ones you like best. What is it about these that appeals to you? Which kinds of pictures would you like to paint or draw?

EXPERIENCES IN APPRECIATION

1. Learn to know other paintings by some of the artists mentioned in this chapter. The references at the end of this book—and your teacher—will help you find examples. Make a report to the class on the artist you select.

2. Select a place and time in your part of the country which you think would be interesting to a landscape painter. Which of the landscape painters studied would you select to make the painting? Would it be a romantic landscape like Corot's, one symbolizing a meaning like Kent's, or a decorative one like Wood's? What features of the landscape would you expect the artist to emphasize?

3. Select a spot in your town which you think would be a good subject for Burchfield to paint; one for Warner to paint. What quality would you expect to see made important in each case?

4. Learn to know other pictures by Rembrandt, especially "The Night Watch" and some of his portraits of old men and women.

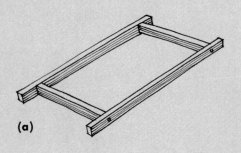

(a)

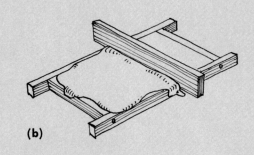

(b)

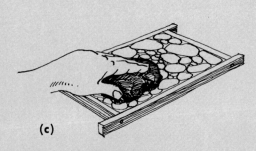

(c)

(a) Make a wood frame about ¾″ high, with inside measurements to match your design. (b) Mix plaster of Paris by pouring plaster into water and stirring continuously. The consistency should be like thick cream. Coat your frame and a flat piece of glass, metal, or wood with soap or oil. Place the frame on the oiled surface and pour the plaster in. Scrape off smooth at once with a board. You may lay a piece of screen wire mesh in the mold before you pour the plaster. This will reinforce the back. (c) Press the pieces of your mosaic into the plaster when it begins to set. Work quickly. Wipe off excess plaster with a damp cloth. Remove frame carefully after plaster has hardened.

5. Create in words an imaginary picture of some dramatic event in modern times that you would like to see painted by Bellows.

6. Try to look at the world through the eyes of an artist. Select the artist who paints as you would like to paint; then try to see parts of your community through his eyes. This would make an interesting class discussion.

7. Visit picture exhibitions at every opportunity.

8. Arrange exhibitions in your school of paintings and drawings by art students.

CREATIVE ACTIVITIES

1. Experiment with water colors or other materials, to describe moods with colors. Refer again to Creative Activities following Chapter Five. You may wish to combine paints with ink, or try other experiments.

2. Paint a series of pictures called "People and Places That I Know." You may change the titles to suit yourself, but begin with familiar places. Street scenes, school activities, or family and friends make good subjects.

Remember that the story a picture tells is very important. Both you and the people who see it when you're finished will enjoy it more. Have a reason for selecting a subject to draw or paint.

3. Create a dramatic picture. Select a truly exciting event from your own experience. Choose colors and contrasts of light and dark that strengthen your idea.

4. Plan a mural for your school. You might wish to refer to the collage on page 195 for ideas. Or you can find places in your community that would make good subjects. Whatever you select should have special meaning.

5. Make a collage of cut or torn paper. Choose your colors carefully. Remember emphasis of main features.

6. Make a mosaic design in plaster. Begin by laying out your materials on a board the same size as your finished piece. When you are satisfied with the design, you can proceed with the next steps.

Use a small frame, about $\frac{3}{4}''$ high, the same size as your design. Mix your plaster rather thin. Spread it to fill the frame. Press the pieces into the plaster after it begins to get firm. When all the pieces are in place you may wish to fill in with more plaster. For some designs you can rub wet plaster into the cracks, then wipe off the excess while it's still soft. Plaster is difficult to clean off an object after it has dried. Never pour plaster in the sink!

Chapter Ten | Beautiful Buildings, Old and New

You have seen that beauty is found in many forms—in machines and posters, in trees and animals, in pictures and statues. Yet there is still another important form in which you may find beauty. It is in buildings. Architecture or the art of building is considered one of the major arts, and it provides a chance to enjoy beauty in one of its finest forms. Buildings, old or new, large or small, public or private, present many opportunities for study and pleasure.

Perhaps when you are older, some of you will become architects. In that case you will read many books and study many years to learn how to plan buildings. Then possibly you will design some of the world's great architecture.

But whether you become an architect or not, you should learn to enjoy beautiful buildings. Since you live in America you should become acquainted with some famous American buildings. This chapter will introduce you to some of them and also to famous buildings in other countries, which are really the ancestors of American buildings.

A Greek Temple— The Parthenon

The first picture on page 200 shows all that is left of an old Greek temple built in Athens and finished in the year 438 B.C. Historians have called this building the most famous in the world, and architects have called it the most perfect building ever built. Time has not dealt kindly with this beautiful old building. As you can see, it is now a ruin, with only the outer columns still standing. The photograph on page 201 will give you a better idea of how the Parthenon looked when it was first constructed. This building, a copy of the

The Greek Parthenon as it appears today.

old Parthenon, was erected in Centennial Park, Nashville, Tennessee. It is used as an art gallery. Naturally it is one of the sights of Nashville. It is worth seeing both for its beauty and for the historical interest in the original Greek building.

The Parthenon was finished in 438 B.C., which means that it is now over 2,400 years old. The temple was intended for the worship of Athena, the favorite and special goddess of the people of Athens. Although the Greek temple was a place of worship, just as our churches today are places of worship, the temple was not planned or used at all like our churches. There

were no seats for people inside the temple, not even a meeting hall. The people were not expected to attend regular services. Usually they stood outside the temple and looked in at the open doorway. On special occasions they were permitted inside, especially if they brought gifts to the goddess.

There were only two rooms in the Parthenon and not even a doorway between. The big room at the eastern end was the sacred room. The Athenians said this room was the earthly home of the goddess. This made it a sacred place, and ordinary humans would not go into a sacred place without a special reason. To do so might anger the goddess! It would be a sacrilege. Instead, people would stand at the open doorway and look at the great golden statue of Athena inside. No wonder people were impressed when they looked into the beautiful room with its marble floor, walls, and columns, and most of all, its great gold statue. The room at the other end of the Parthenon was smaller; here were kept the valuable presents brought by the people to Athena.

The Parthenon was changed into a Christian church about the fifth century. It served as a church for the Christians of Athens for about a thousand years. When the Turks invaded Athens they used it as a mosque. Finally in the seventeenth century the Venetians from the west came to drive the Turks out of Athens. The Turks stored their gunpowder in the Parthenon; when the Venetian general learned of this, he ordered his cannoneers to fire upon the building to destroy the store of gunpowder. Four cannon shots hit the building in rapid succession. There was a tremendous explosion. The Parthenon stood in ruins.

Such a history would make any building famous, but the Parthenon is more famous for its beauty. This might be hard to understand if you could look only at the ruins of the building. However, you can see how it once looked from the picture on this page. It is most famous for its fine proportions. To make the building a bit higher or longer or wider would spoil the "just right" proportions so carefully worked

The Parthenon in Nashville, Tenn., a replica of the old Greek Parthenon.

The Lincoln Memorial in Washington, D.C., is patterned after the Parthenon.

out by those early architects. The columns also seem to fit the building perfectly. They do not give you the feeling that they are merely posts stuck up to support the roof. They are splendid in form and proportion. Notice that each column is wider at the base than at the top, and that the sides curve out very slightly. This makes them graceful and very strong. If they had been made heavier they would have looked clumsy, and if they were perfectly straight they would look stiff.

The triangular space under the roof at each end of the temple is called a *pediment*. In former times the pediments of the Parthenon were filled with beautiful sculpture. The group of statues in each pediment told a story

about the gods, which the ancient Greeks believed. Perhaps you will learn these stories in your history or literature class. The border under the roof all around the building also contained sculptured decoration. The sculptures were separated at regular intervals by three vertical lines. Such groups of lines are called *triglyphs* and the sculptured rectangles between, *metopes*. The triglyphs and metopes are not the same width. Why not?

A Greek Temple in America

At one end of the reflecting pool in Potomac Park, Washington, D.C., stands a splendid memorial to Abraham Lincoln. It is patterned after a Greek temple, and is surrounded by a

202

colonnade of 36 columns, one column for each state in the Union when Lincoln was president. Inside is the great statue of Lincoln by Daniel Chester French with which you became acquainted in your study of famous sculpture, page 134. The impressive statue in its monumental setting makes a shrine which many thousands of Americans visit every year. If you have been there, you will know that people who enter the memorial are so impressed with its beauty and meaning that they stand before it in silence.

Are there any buildings in your town that you think are patterned after a Greek temple?

A Famous Roman Building— The Pantheon

It is said that the Greeks were the great architects and that the Romans were the great builders. The Romans copied designs from Greek architecture but they also used types of construction which the Greeks did not use. The round arch, the dome, and the vault were frequently used in Roman architecture. In your history class you probably learned about the great aqueducts which brought mountain spring water to Rome. These were supported by a series of round stone arches. You may also know about the great Roman amphitheater called the Colosseum. It is

The Pantheon, in Rome, Italy.

PHOTOGRAPH BY EWING GALLOWAY, NEW YORK

Monticello, the home of Thomas Jefferson, is Romanlike in character.

an elliptical building with three tiers of arched openings all around.

The Pantheon, page 203, is one of the world's truly impressive buildings. It was originally built as a temple to all the gods, but was later made into a Christian church. As you can see, it was constructed with a great dome. To support this dome, the walls were built twenty feet thick. There are no windows, and light is admitted only through a circular opening in the center of the dome. People who visit this building are impressed with its great size and spaciousness. They marvel at the Romans who 2,000 years ago could build such a structure.

Do you know any bridges in America that resemble the aqueduct? Or any stadium that resembles the Colosseum? Or any buildings with domes?

Roman Buildings in America

You know from your study of history that Thomas Jefferson was a great statesman as well as the third president of the United States. Did you also learn that he was a fine architect? He designed several buildings that are still famous for their beauty. One of them is his own home in Virginia. He called it Monticello, meaning "little mountain," because it was built on top of a big hill which he leveled off for the building. Jefferson spent several years in France and there came to admire Greek and Roman architecture. When he returned to this country he used these styles in the buildings he designed. Monticello, shown on page 204, has a Roman dome over the center part of the house. Perhaps it does not seem truly Roman, because he was forced to use brick instead of the white marble which the Romans used. However, it is Roman-like in its style.

Jefferson also designed the buildings for the University of Virginia. In fact, the university was his idea; he believed in education for everyone. The Roman influence can be seen in the university buildings too, even more strongly than in Monticello.

Is there any building in your town which you think was patterned after Roman architecture?

Classical Architecture in America

In reading about American architecture you will sometimes find a reference to classic styles or the classical influence. You are already acquainted with such styles because Greek and Roman styles are classic. The Lincoln Memorial and Monticello are in classic styles.

Another famous building in a classic style is the Capitol in Washington, D.C. Its beautiful dome dominates the great mass of the building below. Every American knows this building and likes it, not only because it is impressive but because it stands for our way of govern-

The Capitol building in Washington, D.C.

PHOTOGRAPH BY EWING GALLOWAY, NEW YORK

205

ment. It is a symbol of our great country. Thousands of people visit it each year, so perhaps you have stood on the wide marble steps leading to the great entrance portico and the impressive rotunda (round room) under the dome.

Until just recently classic styles were used for nearly all government buildings in Washington and elsewhere. Someone said that we can hardly govern without a dome! Of course, this is only a joke, for there are many fine government buildings without domes. Later on in the chapter you'll learn about recent changes that have taken place in architecture.

Are many government buildings in your state built in classic style? Ask the history teacher to help you learn the story of the National Capitol, how it was built, who designed it, and other interesting features.

The National Gallery of Art in Washington is a recent building in classic style. It was opened to the public in 1941, but it was designed in a style that was originated more than 2,000 years ago. Below you can see the entrance to the National Gallery. It is similar in appearance to the front of the Pantheon, page 203. The gallery also has a great rotunda which again is similar to the Pantheon. This building houses one of the world's great collections of old masterpieces of painting and sculpture. It seems suitable that a historic style of architecture was selected for a building which contains an important collection of historic art.

What style of architecture was used for the art galleries and museums in your community?

Styles in Buildings Change, But Not Often

Styles in architecture change, but not nearly so often as the styles in women's clothing. We expect new styles in clothing every year, but not in buildings. In the past, architectural styles lasted for several hundred years. There would be minor variations, but the general style would remain the same. The Greek

The National Gallery of Art in Washington, D.C., is patterned after the Roman Pantheon.

The cloistered courtyard from the old monastery at Saint Michel-de-Cuxa in France, which has been moved and reconstructed in New York City.

style lasted at least 500 years. The Roman style which followed it (and partly copied it) also lasted for many hundreds of years. After the fall of the Roman Empire in 476 A.D. there was not much building in Europe for 800 years. Most people were poor and lived unhappy, miserable lives. You may know this period as the Dark Ages. Under such conditions there could not be much fine building. Such great structures as were erected were mostly churches or other religious buildings.

The Romanesque Style

Many churches and other structures have been more or less copied from the Roman style, and so they are called Romanesque (Roman-esk'), meaning Roman-like. The Roman style included round arches, domes, columns, and porticos. Romanesque copied these features and added such items as towers, courtyards, and cloisters. The picture on this page shows the famous Cuxa Cloister. A cloister is a passageway between a row of columns and a wall. The word cloister is also used as a name for a courtyard surrounded by walls. Monasteries and convents are sometimes called cloisters. The Cuxa Cloister is the courtyard from the old monastery at Saint Michel-de-Cuxa in southwestern France. This is a restoration which is located in the museum in New York City known as "The Cloisters." Parts of the ruined Cuxa Cloister in France were brought to New York, and other parts were made in the same style so that the cloister could be reconstructed as accurately as possible.

The Romanesque style has been used in America, although not so much as the classic Roman. Some famous Romanesque buildings in this country are the statehouse in Albany, New York, the courthouse at Pittsburgh, and Trinity Church in Boston. A number of churches in America are Romanesque in style. Perhaps there are some in your town.

The Gothic Style—Then and Now

After roughly 800 years of Romanesque, a new style in architecture appeared. This was in the thirteenth century. You can see what this style was like in the picture on this page, which shows a view of Notre Dame Cathedral in Paris. At first people didn't like this new style in buildings. They were satisfied with the buildings they were used to, and they made fun of the new style, saying it looked as if the Goths had done it. The Goths, as you know, were barbarians who roamed the plains of Europe and were not smart enough to build a great cathedral which would stand strong and beautiful. So when people called the new style Gothic, they meant it was barbaric. But they soon changed their minds and grew to like this strange new style of building. The name was never changed. It is still called Gothic.

You should know a few of the im-

The Notre Dame Cathedral in Paris, France.

Two gargoyles (left) and a grotesque figure (right) from Notre Dame Cathedral in Paris.

portant characteristics of the Gothic style. These features can be seen in the picture of Notre Dame Cathedral.

The arches were pointed. This is quite different from the round arches of the Romanesque style.

Spires and turrets were added to the roof. The towers on the facade (face) were meant to be finished with spires, but so many years passed before the cathedral was completed that they were never added.

The walls were supported by flying buttresses. The purpose of these graceful arched supports was to brace the main wall at the top and keep it from buckling outward from the weight of the roof. Remember there was no steel construction to strengthen buildings in those days. The Romans built the walls of the Pantheon twenty feet thick to support the roof!

Stained glass and traceried windows were introduced. Stone framework surrounded the great windows, which were made of colored glass. Many of these beautiful windows told stories from the Bible. Others formed intricate, geometrical patterns.

The eaves of the roof were decorated with gargoyles and grotesques. Examples of these odd little figures, found on many Gothic cathedrals, are shown in the picture above. The figures in the first picture are really decorative rain spouts, and serve to carry away the rainwater from the roof. The figures are elongated so that the water will not fall too near the wall. You can see the troughs and open mouths through which the water runs. Because of the gurgling noise made by the water, these figures are called gargoyles. The grotesque figure in the second picture is not a rain spout, but was probably designed to frighten off evil spirits in

The Heinz Chapel, University of Pittsburgh; a modern building in the Gothic style.

which superstitious people of the Middle Ages believed.

Remember that the old Gothic cathedrals were built entirely from stone. There are thousands of Gothic buildings in the America today, but most of them were built over a steel framework. One of these is the Heinz Chapel, on page 210. This little chapel is patterned after the famous church in Paris called San Chapelle. It has been said that Gothic spires reach to Heaven. Don't you think this is true of the beautiful spire on the Heinz Chapel? Notice how the turrets echo the skyward thrust.

The Revival of an Old Style— The Renaissance

For about 200 years the Gothic style was used for practically all important buildings. Then in the fifteenth century another style became popular. But it was not an entirely new style—it was really a revival of the old classic styles. It imitated Greek and Roman architecture. This new style was called Renaissance, which means rebirth. In other words, the Renaissance style was a rebirth of the Greek and Roman styles. However, it used the old classic styles in a new way and is really a distinct style.

The Riccardi Palace in Florence, Italy, is a Renaissance building of the fifteenth century. It is pictured on this page. Some people think it looks more like a prison than a palace, but in the days when it was built rich men needed strong houses in which to keep their

The Riccardi Palace, built in Florence, Italy during the Renaissance.

211

valuable possessions. It was their protection against robbers and against mobs belonging to another political party.

The Georgian Style— Really Renaissance

Georgian is the name given to Renaissance architecture in England. It was called Georgian because it was popular during the period when kings George I, George II, and George III were rulers. It was also during this period that the American colonies were growing and developing. Plans and drawings of English Georgian architecture were brought to America, and the natural result was Georgian buildings in the American colonies. You see how, by a roundabout way, Renaissance architecture reached America. It is called Georgian Colonial, or more often just Colonial.

Probably you are already familiar with the most famous Georgian Colonial building in America. It is Independence Hall in Philadelphia. A picture of this building is on page 213. Here the Declaration of Independence was signed, and here you see the Liberty Bell which rang so hard that it cracked. Of course, you have learned its story in your history class. This Renaissance style does not look much like the Italian Renaissance buildings—for instance, the Riccardi Palace. Georgian Colonial was made to suit the needs of the place where it was built. It could not be great and pretentious like the churches of Europe, and it need not be so prisonlike as the Riccardi Palace. Yet you can see the same features used in another way. The windows are regularly spaced, and the building is symmetrical in form. Balustrades decorate the top of the building. The tower has a dome-like top, and round arches are used in the tower openings.

You are probably acquainted with other Colonial buildings through your history study. Mount Vernon, home of George Washington, is one of the most famous. It is visited by thousands of people every year.

There may be examples of Colonial architecture in your community. Are they historic or modern copies?

Spanish Mission Architecture in America

Most Colonial architecture is found in the eastern part of the United States. This is natural, because that is where the British colonies were. Another type of architecture is common in the southwestern part of the country, and it is interesting to know why it is there. Mexico and some of our present southwestern states were first settled by the Spanish. Later, about the time the Revolutionary War was being fought in the East, the Franciscan monks were building missions in California. These missions were something like the monasteries of the Middle Ages, with the church and other buildings grouped about a cloistered court. The Franciscans built a chain of these missions

Independence Hall in Philadelphia.

213

along the seacoast, a day's journey apart. The old mission at Santa Barbara is shown at the top of this page. These missions were built of adobe, or sun-dried brick. Generally, the mission had one or two towers with round, arched openings. In the Santa Barbara Mission the towers are crowned with domes. Notice the interesting step divisions in the towers, graduated from the largest at the bottom to the smallest at the top. This makes a pleasing variety of proportions.

Many buildings in California and in other parts of the Southwest have been designed in this architectural style. Courthouses, libraries, post offices, and thousands of homes show the Spanish influence. It is natural that the people of the Southwest would choose a style of architecture that is important historically to the area. It is not only beautiful, but well suited to the climate. Small windows shut out the glaring sunlight, and the patios and courtyards make pleasant outdoor living places.

You may remember from your study of American history that the Spanish also settled in Florida during the early days of this country. There are many buildings in the Spanish style throughout that state.

Ask your social studies teacher to help you learn the story of Fort Marion at St. Augustine, Florida.

Modern Styles of Architecture

New styles in architecture don't happen very often. In this chapter you have skipped rapidly over the centuries since the days of the ancient Greeks and found only six different architectural styles used in western Europe and in America. They were Greek, Roman, Romanesque, Gothic, Renaissance, and Spanish Mission. Of course there were many variations of these styles—so many that they cannot be discussed here. Later you will probably learn about other styles used in eastern Europe, Asia, and northern Africa.

To finish this discussion of architectural styles you will learn about the one that is developing in your own time. Tall buildings are still very new in the world of architecture, so their style is called *modern*. You may well wonder what it will be called 2,000 years from now. Perhaps it will be known as "Twentieth Century" or the "American Style."

In the beginning the new architecture did not have a style of its own. The first skyscraper, built in Chicago in 1890, was made to resemble a classical building. In fact, most skyscrapers were at first decorated with Greek columns, domes, or Gothic trimmings. This was not good, because skyscrapers are not adapted to the same kind of materials or construction methods as the historic styles. Skyscrapers depend on structural steel for their strength. Ornate columns and heavy stone door frames are not needed for support. If they are added for decoration, they must be hung from the steel frame. Classical style buildings were built strictly from the ground up, with everything below supporting what was above it. With skyscrapers, however, the framework may be many stories high before exterior work even begins.

For still another reason the old styles are not best for the skyscraper. Architects say that the exterior should not conceal the way a building is made. Therefore the exterior of a skyscraper should suggest the steel structure underneath. Historic styles do not do this.

After some years of experimenting with this new and almost limitless structural method, architects developed the modern skyscraper. On page 216 is the group of buildings at Rockefeller Center, New York City. it is easy to feel that underneath the stone and concrete are great steel columns and beams which support the structure. There are no decorations or cornices to disturb the clean sweep of the surface. Vertical and horizontal structural members and the rows of windows form striking patterns of dark against light. The setbacks

Rockefeller Center in New York City. The tallest structure is the RCA building.

vertical members clean and unbroken. He added interest by changing the proportions of horizontal members. The lower photograph shows that the architect extended the vertical members beyond the surface to create strong shadow patterns. These projections also serve to shade the offices inside at certain times during the day.

The extended walkway cover which dominates the upper photograph serves a double purpose. It covers the ground level walkway, and in good weather it acts as an open air passage from one building to another. Its simple, light construction is like that of the buildings it connects.

What other kinds of walkways have you learned about in this chapter?

or steps in the buildings were required by city building ordinances, but they too add interest.

It was mentioned above that the exterior design of a building should suggest the structural members within. A design which achieves this is sometimes called *functional*. You'll recall that the same term was used in describing automobiles, washers, and other man-made objects. The closeup pictures on this page show the functional style in a modern building. The top photograph may be considered an excellent example. The appearance of this building is dependent upon the way it was constructed. But the architect arranged these structural members to create a handsome building. He emphasized the height of the building by leaving the

217

Modern buildings are functional inside and out. Thick walls and heavy ceilings have given way to lightweight wall panels and luminous ceilings. The office pictured above is a pleasant place to work. The ceiling is made of preformed plastic panels lighted from above. The walls are light, and painted in soft colors. Doors and natural wood panels add a touch of elegance to the overall appearance. The furniture is functional too, and constructed of the same wood as the doors and panels above them. Do you think this style of architecture and decorative treatment would be suitable for a school building?

The building you just studied was built very recently. Things that are being built now—buildings, chairs, and in fact anything—are called *contemporary*. It is no surprise that functional and contemporary are almost synonymous terms. This is true because today's leading designs are functional.

Functional or contemporary architecture has indeed found its way into school buildings. The two views of the new Azalea Junior High School in Pinellas County, Florida, are exciting

Azalea Junior High School, Pinellas County, Florida.

219

evidence that schoolhouses need not all look alike. Similarly, courthouses need not have the uninspiring look that so many of them have. Gasoline stations could be different and better too. A building should be designed first of all to suit a particular purpose. Isn't this what function means? The school pictured is both functional and beautiful. It is built of steel, with lightweight cast panels attached to the outside of the frame. The building is light in color and reflects the heat of the sun, an important consideration in this climate. The panels shield the rooms from direct sunlight, adding to the comfort of the students inside. Many buildings like this one are built with transluscent roof panels that admit soft, diffused light on even the brightest days.

In Chapter Two, Automobiles, Airplanes, and Art, you learned about repetition of forms that create pleasing patterns. A repetition of forms is called *rhythm*, just as a repetition of notes establishes rhythm in music. The school pictured here is a splendid example of this important principle of design. All parts appear to fit together in exactly the right way—and they are simply designed, beautifully proportioned, and inviting. Compare this building with your own school. Can you identify the architectural style of your school?

Buildings That Belong to the Landscape

In the next chapter you'll see a famous building by Frank Lloyd Wright,

Red Rock Theater, near Denver, Colorado.

DEPARTMENT OF PARKS AND RECREATION, CITY AND COUNTY OF DENVER

a home in the hills of Pennsylvania. It too belongs to the landscape.

Other architects have taken advantage of natural formations in the landscape to build structures of various kinds. The photograph on page 220 is a view of the Red Rock Theater near Denver, Colorado. This giant amphitheater was built between two natural rock walls, and faces a natural rock sounding board. The huge rocks on either side are red sandstone. Most of the rock out-croppings in the area are the same color. A large part of the construction was done with stone cut from the same material. There are seventy rows of seats on this hillside. Stretched end to end, they would reach nearly $2\frac{1}{2}$ miles. The stage is 60 feet deep and 100 feet wide. What an impressive sight it is!

The beautiful church on this page is "Chapel of the Holy Cross," located in Arizona. It was designed by Ashen and Allen, a well known architectural firm.

In recent years, an increasing number of architects have learned to take advantage of the natural landscape, adapting their structures to formations of earth and rock. This handsome building appears to grow out of the rugged landscape, and looks as strong as the rocks themselves. Explain why the flat, tapered sides of the building and the massive cross are well suited to this location. Why did the architects choose the color you see in the cast concrete structure?

PHOTO BY MIKE AND LYNN SIMS

Only a Beginning

The modern style of architecture—the American style—is only just beginning. The periods of architecture you have read about began before 438 B.C.—over 2,400 years ago. The style that dominates American architecture today is less than eighty years old! Yet its influence is world wide. Since World War II, architects and builders from nations large and small have studied the technology of American architectural engineering. The result is evident in photographs of beautiful new buildings in the functional style, all around the world. The American style is here to stay!

Experiences in Appreciation

1. Select a style of architecture which was used in the period of history which you are studying. Ask your history teacher's co-operation in studying the life of the period. Try to find out why buildings were built as they were.

2. Arrange an excursion to see the finest architecture in your community. Be sure to find out when each building was completed.

3. Study and report on your favorite style of architecture.

4. Plan some criticism lessons on the architecture in your community. Remember that criticism includes good as well as bad comments.

5. Arrange a program for an architect to visit your school and speak to you about building styles in your town, or about trends in modern architecture.

Creative Activities

1. Design the facade of a building in functional style. Keep in mind what use would be made of the building.

2. Make some sketches of the buildings in your community which you think represent good examples of an architectural style.

3. Model a grotesque figure. You may use clay, papier maché, or wood. Your project should be part of a larger study, perhaps a group project.

4. You have seen that inside design is as important as outside. Redesign your classroom in a way that suits its use better.

5. Plan a color and lighting scheme for a room in your school. You may wish to refer to the examples of interior design on pages 218 and 238.

<table>
<tr><td>Chapter
Eleven</td><td># Art Begins at Home</td></tr>
</table>

A search for beauty may lead you to many places. For those who have learned to see it, there is beauty in the trees, the sky and the sea, in art galleries and public parks, in shops, theaters, and schools. But the search should really begin at home. It is here that you have the most frequent opportunities to create and enjoy beautiful things. An attractive home may mean much more to you than the great masterpieces of art in all the world's galleries, because it is a part of your personal life. The house and its setting, the furniture you use, and the clothes you wear can give you pleasure every day. Even the food that your mother prepares and the way she sets it on the table can be attractive. Meals that look good usually taste good.

Probably you like to buy useful and decorative items for your room. Someday you may buy furnishings for your own home, and arrange them according to your tastes. When you do these things you become an artist. Some people are poor artists and some are good. Whether you manage to create an attractive home or not depends on whether you have learned to use the things you have, and how to choose wisely when you buy something new. You can't learn much about home decoration in one chapter, but what you have learned in preceding chapters will help you to deal with this special problem in art.

Putting Things Together— Large and Small

No matter how good looking your furniture, rugs, lamps, pictures, and other furnishings, your home will not really be attractive and comfortable to live in unless these furnishings are arranged to the best advantage. If your dresser top is loaded with articles

223

This living room invites you to relax.

shoved together in helter-skelter fashion, these objects will lose their attractiveness. If the furniture is placed as though it were being shown off in a store window instead of for use in a home, it will lose its charm. If pictures are hung just to break up a blank wall, not as part of a planned grouping, and if flowers are jammed into vases instead of carefully arranged, you won't be using them to best advantage.

Remember that good arrangement doesn't require the expenditure of money. Generally it means making the best of what you have. Whether the furnishings are beautiful or homely, they'll look better if properly arranged. What is the best approach to this problem of good arrangement?

The arrangement of furniture and accessories in the living room on this page can best be described as inviting. The furniture was selected to suit the style and size of the room—that is, purchased to fit a particular space. The simple, clean lines of the furniture are well suited to the simplicity of the room itself. The emphasis in this contemporary setting is on horizontal lines. The fireplace, chairs and sofas, and the coffee table echo the horizontal. Low furniture with smooth wood frames is characteristic of the contemporary style. This furniture design is especially suited to today's homes because ceilings are lower and walls are usually smooth with little or no added decoration. But the important thing about this room is that it says "Welcome." A good arrangement can be a welcome sign in your home too.

A Decorator Is an Artist

You have seen how an artist composes a picture. He arranges the parts in such a way that they appear to belong together. He emphasizes certain parts to create further interest in them, to make you enjoy what you see. When you arrange the furnishings in your home you're putting things together too, and a successful result depends upon how well you select and arrange the parts. Decorating a home means making it as *attractive* as possible, and it should be *functional* too. It's easy to remember those two requirements.

Color, proportion, and function are terms already familiar to you. They are important considerations in making your home more attractive. The rooms shown on pages 226 and 227 are both beautiful and comfortable. Comfort is the primary function of furniture. The furniture in both rooms is functional— designed to do a particular job well. And artistically, the individual pieces in both settings are well proportioned and attractive in color and shape.

There Are Two Sides to Every Story

How often have you heard someone say, "There are two sides to every story"? People are complex. Every time a new style car, a changed hemline, or a faster bike is made, someone

will say, "That's the only thing to have. The rest are old fashioned!" Well, this has been going on since John Caveman told his father that times had changed, and that he should get with the rest of the crowd. But John's father was like some of us. He had a few things around the cave that *his* father had used, and he liked them. Not only that, he planned to make a few more exactly like those he had, and give them to his relatives. Of course you know what John's father was up to. He intended to convince as many people as he could that the new generation had developed some ideas that were simply ridiculous. Imagine using wood for furniture when the whole house was full of rock benches! There were some folks who agreed, and they continued living in the traditional way.

But young John's ideas were sound too. "Why not try something different?" he asked. "Look. I can carry my stool!" His might have been the first contemporary style, since it was up to date! You can be certain this tale has no basis in historical fact, but it does serve to point out that both old and new methods can be based on sound notions.

Fortunately, people today are not in the predicament that John and his father were in. Most furniture made today is comfortable, but none of theirs was. So whether you prefer traditional or contemporary styling, you will sit in comfort. Your choice will depend primarily on appearance, with a great deal of inside help from your personality.

SIMMONS, MAKERS OF HIDE-A-BED SOFA

A Traditional Setting

The picture on this page shows a very impressive living room furnished in traditional style. The emphasis in this room is on the davenport and the decorative wall arrangement above. The matching tables, chairs, and lamps create a pleasing, formal arrangement. The flowers, books, and pewter shown against the dark green background add glamour to the room.

The arrangement of the furniture invites one to come and enjoy a pleasant hour. The color scheme is worked out in tones of red, yellow, and green. You learned in Chapter Five that warm colors create a feeling of vitality. Decorators know how colors affect people,

and use them to suit the purpose of the room and the personalities of the people who will use it.

Now compare this room and furniture style with the contemporary setting on the opposite page.

A Contemporary Living Room

The beautiful living room on page 227, designed in contemporary style, gives you a feeling of spaciousness not evident in the traditional room. This effect is produced chiefly by the use of large areas of flat color—the off-white ceiling, walls, and floor covering. The low furniture with its straight-line design reflects the same scheme—areas of solid color. Yet the setting appears as elegant as the traditional room. This effect has been achieved by using rich colors in small areas to make the room sparkle. These two rooms might be compared to two dresses. One has a fine overall pattern, like printed silk. The other is plain, accented by only a few pieces of sparkling jewelry.

The emphasis in this room is on the fireplace grouping, with the accent on the raised black hearth and fireplace. The color plan is simple, based on tones of red and orange. The light walls and rug make a handsome background for the reds and blacks of the furniture and fireplace.

Another Look at Contemporary Furnishings

Contemporary design has often been called functional design. This is gener-

ally true, although the words *contemporary* and *functional* do not have the same meaning. Even the caveman had functional furniture. Frequently when man has needed something he couldn't find, he has made it. Usually the simplest of tools and furniture are the most functional. Their shape, weight, size, and often color too, are dictated by the use to be made of the article. Functional design is a product of need. But it can be most attractive too.

Pictured on the next few pages are a number of ordinary things you would find in any home. Look at them as individual pieces and also as they are used with other furnishings or accessories, then make your own judgment of the contemporary style before reading the text which follows.

227

PITTSBURGH PLATE GLASS COMPANY

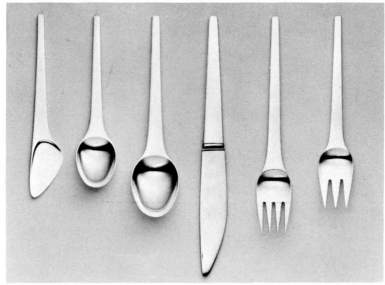

Pure function! The stainless tableware and white china pictured here were designed for one purpose—to use when eating. But it's no accident that they are beautifully shaped. Their designers were aware of the beauty of clean line and good proportion.

SILVER PITCHER AND SERVICE. COURTESY OF
THE ARTIST, ALFRED H. WARDLE

*The silver pitcher and three-piece service
were hammered from flat silver sheets. They
are basically simple, with decorative knobs
and handles added. These are functional
pieces. Explain this.*

*The mahogany bowl and plate suit the material well—smooth sur-
faces, no projections to break off. Their handsome proportions and
natural oil finish add both beauty and usefulness.*

COLLECTION, THE MUSEUM OF MODERN ART, NEW YORK. GIFT OF DOROTHY LIEBES

229

A simple flower vase. The fluted surface accents the vertical shape. This design would be suitable for arrangements of flowers as well.

Good design isn't limited to vases and plates. Vinegar, mustard—even after-shave lotion—find their way into the industrial designer's assignment schedule. These containers are well suited to their purposes —easy to hold and hard to tip.

A hand-ground crystal bowl of beautiful shape. The refractive quality of the crystal provides the only "decoration"—and it's just enough.

A pottery figurine that would fit any furnishing style. Many people collect figurines. Look for pieces that suit the material from which they are made. Refer to page 91.

231

Contemporary furniture in the functional style. Both pieces are basic box shapes with smooth, uncluttered surfaces, well-designed storage areas and natural finishes that are easy to care for. Space underneath makes for easy room cleaning. These are standard items, machine-made. Don't you agree that a square-cornered box with conveniently divided spaces is the best storage unit? That's the carefully planned function of these chests.

JENS RISOM DESIGN, INC.

KNOLL ASSOCIATES, INC.

A lightweight, extra chair for the living room or dining room. This is a handcrafted piece, with smoothly contoured sections that blend naturally together. The woven cane seat is comfortable and flexible.

GEORG JENSEN, INC.

This is one of our "pets." Here we must use that word function again! Remember what it means? This seat was designed to do a specific job in the best possible way. It's just what we need for an extra-light comfortable chair-for-anywhere. Want to move it? Just pick it up by the handles and take it away.

Jens Risom Design, Inc.

*Beauty in a home begins at the front door. The entrance hall should say
"Welcome" to anyone who comes inside—and this includes those who live there.
This entry is functional all the way—from the easy-to-care-for natural slate floor
to the open-air stairs leading to the second floor. The chest will hold mail, keys,
perhaps extra gloves or a scarf. And don't overlook the hooked-yarn wall hanging.
Would you like to plan a color scheme for this entry?*

Beauty at Breakfast— And Dinner, Too

You wouldn't ordinarily think of art when you're hungry, but you can enjoy it with your breakfast—and dinner too. You can be sure that Mother and Dad thought about it when they selected the china, silver, and many other things in your home. You are pleased, as everyone is, when the table is set attractively. Every dish and fork, the cream pitcher and glassware, even the napkins, can make your table more attractive. It doesn't matter whether they came from the dime store or the most exclusive shop in town—they can be good looking at any price. So why shouldn't you enjoy a bit of beauty with your cereal, and with pork chops too?

There are literally hundreds of designs for silverware alone! And there are just as many choices available in dishes, salad bowls, and vases. No matter what you may look for, you'll be astounded at the number of different styles. When you are called upon someday to select your own, you should be prepared to make intelligent choices.

Think About the Extras

Little things in a house tell a lot about the people who live there. Flowers, vases and bowls, figurines and hobby collections, are all personal notes on the family. The pewter collection displayed in the setting on page 226 demonstrates how the personal touch adds interest to a room arrangement. Explain how the collection of books in the living room on page 227 does the same. The things you choose as accessories should appeal to you personally. Why not make the most of this opportunity to make your home look comfortable and lived-in?

The accessories, on pages 228 to 231, may not be the ones you would choose, but all of them would fit a contemporary setting—even though the styles seem to be mixed. You can find accessories to suit your own taste in furniture and department stores.

The Basic Furnishings

A large part of the money spent on a home is for furniture. You will want to choose these pieces carefully because they are expected to last a long time. In the beginning, decide whether you want a traditional or contemporary style. The style you select will set the scheme for the other things you buy. Remember that everything in your home should look as if it belonged there. Of course, many accessories can fit in with any style.

A few pieces of contemporary furniture and several room settings are illustrated on pages 234 and 236. All of the furniture is functional. You will find it to be clean in design and light in appearance. Compare these pieces with the furniture in the traditional room on page 226. What are the major differences between the two styles?

235

Jens Risom Design, Inc.

These are two important rooms. Their purposes dictate their arrangements—a traffic lane all around the table, and convenient silver and linen storage. And for the bedroom, "quiet" design and convenient storage. Both rooms have light furniture, well off the floor. This makes cleaning an easier task.

The Kitchen Is a Place to Work

Probably the most frequently used room in your home is the kitchen. Your mother may spend half of her working day there, so it should be well designed and cheerful. A cheerful kitchen is often the meeting place when friends drop in. When you arrive home from school, don't you often "report in" to the kitchen?

Of all the rooms in the home, the kitchen should be the most carefully planned. The plan must be functional, responding to the working habits of your mother and to the living habits of the rest of the family. For example, if your mother enjoys cooking a variety of dishes and likes to bake pies and cakes, she'll need plenty of work space. If your family enjoys eating in the kitchen, you'll need a table or counter for this as well. If your family is large, you'll need more storage space for dishes, foods, pots and pans, and the many kitchen accessories that accumulate as if by magic. And of course, a large family needs a larger refrigerator and a larger range.

Another important matter is the arrangement of appliances to save steps. A well designed, functional kitchen can save your mother many steps every day, adding up to miles over the months. The kitchen on page 238 is an excellent example of beauty combined with function. The practical features of this kitchen do more than save steps. The hard-surfaced counter tops are easy to clean. Cabinets are smooth, deep, and arranged for various kinds of storage. The table is available for double duty —eating or preparing food. And the floor, made of non-slip glazed tile, is as practical as the rest of the room. Anything spilled here, or tracked in from outside, would not be a disaster.

The color scheme of this contemporary kitchen is as handsome as the fixtures. The soft yellow tone, the color of the walls, cabinets, and floor, was a wise choice because it reflects a soft light and makes a background that allows other colors to "show off." The turquoise of the range, refrigerator, and dishwasher become sparkling accents. The lemons in the dish on the counter, the green salad and bottles on the table, the plant by the doorway— all add sparkle, and a personal touch.

Explain why the flat-surfaced units are especially suitable for a room where cooking is going on.

Even the Laundry

Why shouldn't a laundry be attractive too? Washing and ironing, sorting and mending, and folding the weekly wash are big jobs. Look how pleasant they could be with color, curtains, and a counter! Compare this functional laundry with your own. Picture your own laundry room paneled with pegboard or plywood, and painted in cheerful colors. Lumber companies today carry "packaged" rooms in stock. These prefinished panels can easily be attached to any existing wall.

238

The General Electric Company

Colonial house in Williamsburg, Virginia.

Art Outside Your Home

Beauty of a house exterior depends on good design, just as does any article of furnishing inside the house. The pictures on this page and page 241 show two very different styles of architecture —both beautiful. The first is an old Colonial house in Williamsburg, Virginia, and the other is a contemporary style house in Minneapolis, Minnesota. Characteristics of Colonial style are a steep roof, small square windowpanes, shutters, white clapboard siding, and red brick chimneys. In the East, where this style originated, the snowfall is heavy; the steep roof causes the snow to slide off. Dormer windows in the roof provide light and ventilation for the upstairs bedrooms. Because there were no furnaces to heat the entire house from a central place, Colonial houses were usually built with several fireplaces. In winter the upstairs bedrooms were very cold, and it was common practice to warm the bed with heated bricks or metal bed-warmers. Sounds chilly, doesn't it? This house was built for function—steep roofs to keep the snow off, dormer windows for light upstairs, small windows and tight shutters for storm protection, large fireplaces for warmth and cooking.

The contemporary house is quite different in design. The roof has only a slight pitch, just enough to drain off the rain water. The roof is built strong enough to hold heavy snow loads. The flat roof of this house permits full use of the upstairs rooms, whereas the Colonial house had sloped walls upstairs. Houses today are well insulated all around. Walls and ceilings are blanketed with materials that hold the heat in, and windows may be double glass. Central heating furnaces, automatically controlled, keep our houses warm on the coldest days of winter. Tight, strong construction in modern houses keeps out drafts that many times chilled the feet of our great grandfathers.

Machine-cut lumber in many standard sizes permits great variety in contemporary design. This was not the case in Colonial times when timbers were hand-hewn and boards hand-sawed one at a time. And in Colonial times, roof shingles, called split shakes, were made by splitting off thin pieces from short lengths of log.

A House That Fits the Ground

Just as certain kinds of furniture fit you best, so should houses fit the ground where they are constructed. A house should look as if it belongs where it is. Some architects carefully design their houses to suit the slope of the land, and to go with the characteristics of the trees and shrubs that are there. On page 242 you see an excellent example of a house that fits the site. The ground is nearly flat, so the house was designed to appear close to it,

A contemporary-style house in Minnesota.

ANDERSEN CORPORATION, BAYPORT, MINNESOTA

241

A house that fits the ground.

creating a horizontal, rather than vertical, appearance. This was achieved by accenting the horizontal structural members, such as the roof and low front wall. On the other hand, the vertical lines were made inconspicuous. To do this, the architect used metal columns in the front of the house. They are scarcely noticeable. The thin columns with lacy grillwork next to them suggest the growth pattern of the trees, the columns repeating the straight, thin verticals of the trunks, and the grillwork reflecting the leaf pattern. The high, handsome wall in front of the house, with its open, leaflike design, also helps relate the house to the ground.

The photograph on page 243 shows the area behind the front wall. The roof is cut out to permit the sunlight to enter. Notice how the wall blends with the shrubs and trees. A study of the plan on page 243 indicates that the large glass doors open from the bedrooms onto the little court.

In its general idea and plan, this contemporary house is very different from the traditional. It has an "open" arrangement. Rooms are not divided by solid walls and doorways; large glass areas bring the outdoors into the house. Sliding doors that open onto patios or gardens are as commonplace today as chimneys.

Garden area outside bedrooms. Plants grow all year round in this protected, sunny spot.

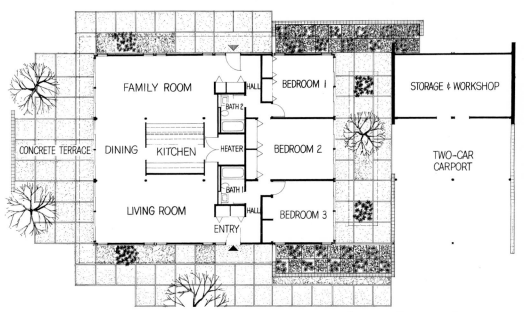

243

Design in Your Planting

The planting of flowers and shrubs as a part of the overall design can help relate the house to its site, and at the same time make it much more attractive. A house with no planting around it looks unfinished. Foundation planting and other shrubs that are planned to harmonize with the house add interest to the whole plan. Builders who are aware of this are careful to protect existing growth, and they may add other plants after the house is completed. How often have you seen a development where the builder began by removing all trees and bushes before starting construction?

In the next picture you'll see a house that is so well related to the site that it looks as if it grew there.

A World-Famous House

The remarkable house on the rocky hillside is "Fallingwater," located at Ohiopyle, Pennsylvania. It is a masterpiece of architecture by the late Frank Lloyd Wright, long the nation's most influential architect. Wright was famous for his imaginative uses of concrete and steel, and for his ability to take advantage of the natural landscape in designing his structures. This house appears to be an extension of the rock ledges upon which it is built. Trees and natural shrubs remain undistributed. The creek flows into a pool beneath the overhanging deck of the level above, then tumbles over the rock ledge to the level below.

The roofs and decks that seem to defy gravity are built of reinforced concrete, the same kind of construction used in skyscrapers. There are no posts under the decks. They are supported instead by steel beams that extend back under the floors or other parts of the structure. You might compare one of these decks or overhanging roofs with a see-saw—a heavier person holding a

"Fallingwater," Ohiopyle, Pennsylvania.

PHOTO COURTESY, LAUREL HIGHLANDS, INC., LIGONIER, PENNSYLVANIA

244

A pleasant little retreat in a city backyard.

lighter one off the ground. This is called *cantilever construction*. Wright used the cantilever method on other buildings too, both large and small.

Describe in your own words how the natural stone chimney and walls help relate the house to the ground. Why do the cantilevered decks and roofs seem to belong?

Outside Living Is Fun

A house can be more attractive and more fun to live in when you extend your living area outside. Shrubs and trees help "tie the house to the ground," but this is not the only way you can benefit from the grounds around your home. For fullest enjoyment, set aside an area that will become an "outside living room." It may be a paved patio, a shrub-bordered private yard, or a small garden. No matter what the size, or whether or not it is paved, it should be an extension of the living area of your house. You might easily get to know it as your daily vacation area. If you enjoy trees, flowers and fresh air, why not take advantage of them whenever you wish? Some sturdy patio furniture and provisions for lighting the area at night can turn a backyard into a beautiful, private retreat.

The small garden pictured on this page is the backyard retreat of a Pennsylvania family. Bushes along the street end keep it private. Many a hamburger has been grilled here! Is there a place outside your house that could be made as inviting as this one is?

An Assignment for You

Continue your study of architecture and furniture styles. Be on the lookout for furniture that is functional and beautiful. Help your family arrange your home and furnishings to be practical and beautiful. If you can, prepare a color scheme for a new spring paint job.

EXPERIENCES IN APPRECIATION

1. Collect pictures of the kind of furniture you would like for your room. Plan your room around the things you do there—homework, your hobby, entertaining a close friend, and of course sleeping.

2. Study pictures of house exteriors, and select the type you like best. Is your choice traditional or contemporary? Explain how either style can be functional.

3. Plan an outside living area for your home. Use photographs to demonstrate how you would plant it.

4. Arrange a trip to a museum. Study the styles of home furnishings you see there. Hold a class discussion on the things you saw.

5. Collect pictures of wall arrangements, furniture, gardens or patios, houses, designs for wall coverings, or any material which can be discussed and criticized for art quality.

CREATIVE ACTIVITIES

1. Collect pictures of furniture in several different styles. Analyze them for function and decorative qualities.

2. Design several pieces of contemporary furniture. Consider both beauty and function.

3. Develop a color scheme for your home. Include draperies, wall finishes, and rugs, as well as furniture.

4. Make a collage or painting for a contemporary home. Relate the colors to those in the room. Would a painting in the Romantic style suit a contemporary setting?

5. Construct wire or clay sculptures that would be suitable for use in your own home.

6. Redesign your own room. Arrange the furniture to best advantage. Refer to Chapter One, Experiences in Appreciation.

7. Make a model of a contemporary house. Use stiff paper board. Paint windows, doors, and outside finish on the board. You may thicken edges of roofs with balsa wood. Plan the area surrounding the house, using small pieces of sponge for shrubs and trees.

Chapter Twelve | Keep the World Beautiful

The Grand Canyon in Arizona, pictured on page 248, is one of America's unspoiled areas. There are thousands of other beautiful places to visit in our country—the rolling hills of the East, the lakes of the North and the plains of the Midwest, the pine woods and historic plantations of the South, the rugged mountains, deserts and evergreen forests of the West. Do you suppose they will always be there for Americans to enjoy?

This is a chapter with a moral. It "preaches" at you, and tells you what you should do. You may not like it, but anyway it is a short chapter. It has just one idea—your responsibility for keeping the world beautiful.

You have found beauty in art galleries and homes, in the country and in the city, in man-made objects and in nature. Some of it, like the great statues of Khephren and Abraham Lincoln, is strong and lasting. Some beauty, like that in many fine school buildings, is more easily spoiled. Here is where your responsibility comes in. If you mark on the walls, scratch your initials on the desks, and break down the shrubbery around the building, then you are making ugliness. We know that everyone likes his world to be beautiful, but not everyone helps to keep it that way. Wouldn't you rather attend a clean, attractive school with lawns and shrubs around it, than a dingy one surrounded only by bare ground? Certainly if you are fortunate enough to attend an attractive school, you should feel responsible for keeping it that way.

Here is a true story. A junior high school boy who was talented in art had carved a head from stone. His teacher asked him to bring it to school and

Photo by Mike and Lynn Sims

show the class. It was heavy but he brought it, and also his tools. Before school he was showing it and his tools to some friends. One of them said, "How can you cut stone with a chisel?" The boy said, "I'll show you." They were standing near a statue which decorated the front of the building. With his chisel and hammer, the boy chipped a corner off the base of the statue.

This boy had created a head of some beauty from stone, but he had failed to do his part in keeping his own school building beautiful. You may say that he was just being thoughtless, but this is no excuse for destroying anything.

Some people purposely destroy the things that other people enjoy. The park superintendent of any large city will tell you that thousands of dollars worth of property is destroyed every

WESTERN PENNSYLVANIA CONSERVANCY

year. Benches are tipped over and broken, windows are smashed, statues are defaced, shrubs are trampled and trees are killed by knife cuts in their trunks. Parks are planned for people who cannot afford private parks of their own, yet some of these same people destroy the parks made for them. It's very foolish to ruin the thing that can bring you pleasure.

Most people don't go around deliberately spoiling the attractive things in their homes and communities. But many do it through carelessness. Dirty fingermarks are often left on walls or on the pages of a book. Throwing away school papers on the street is another kind of carelessness. So is trampling across the corner of a lawn when the grass is young and the ground soft.

It's fun to go out into the country and find a pleasant place to eat a picnic lunch. Trees, skies, flowers, grass, and sunshine are there to enjoy. The nicer the spot you can find, the more fun it is. Who could ask for a better place than the one shown on page 249? It's an out-of-the-way little valley in the Pennsylvania woods. Many people have enjoyed a picnic lunch here, and it is still a beautiful place. But some people are careless about the beauty of the woods and other choice picnic spots. You can see on this page what happened to another favorite area when careless picnickers packed up to go back home, and left their litter behind.

Your responsibility for keeping the world beautiful is just the same whether you're in a public park or your own backyard. You will be able to think of dozens of ways in which every boy and girl is responsible for keeping the world a pleasant place to live in.

This is the end of the chapter with a moral—*keep the world beautiful.*

Books for Further Study

Drawing and Painting

Anderson, Doug, *How to Draw with the Light Touch*, Watson-Guptill Publications, Inc., 1954

Bradshaw, Percy V. and Haslehust, Ernest W., *I Wish I Could Draw*, (Studio) The Viking Press, 1945

Lawson, Philip I., *Practical Perspective Drawing*, McGraw-Hill Book Company, 1943

Loomis, Andrew, *Figure Drawing for All It's Worth*, The Viking Press, 1943

Petterson, H. and Gerring, R., *Exploring with Paint*, Reinhold Publishing Corp., 1964

Sorgman, Mayo, *Brush and Palette*, Reinhold Publishing Corp., 1965

Wootton, Frank, *Drawing Aircraft*, (Studio) The Viking Press, 1959

Sculpture and Crafts

Coats, Helen, *Weaving for Amateurs*, second edition, (Studio) The Viking Press, 1946

Cox, Doris and Warren, Barbara, *Creative Hands*, second edition, John Wiley & Sons, Inc., 1951

Detroit Public Schools, *The Use of Clay*, Board of Public Education, Detroit, Publication 386, 1955

Duncan, Julia H. and D'Amico, Victor, *How to Make Pottery and Ceramic Sculpture*, Museum of Modern Art, 1947

Hughes, Toni, *How to Make Shapes in Space*, E. P. Dutton & Co., 1955

Karasz, Mariska, *Adventures in Stitches and More Adventures—Less Stitches*, Funk & Wagnalls Co., 1959

Kenny, John B., *Ceramic Sculpture*, Chilton Co., 1953

Moseley, S., Johnson, P., and Koenig, H., *Crafts Design*, Wadsworth Publishing Co., 1962

Read, Herbert, *The Art of Sculpture*, Pantheon — Random House, 1964

Rood, John, *Sculpture in Wood*, University of Minnesota, 1950

Röttger, Ernst, *Creative Clay Design*, Reinhold Publishing Corp., 1962

———, *Creative Paper Design*, Reinhold Publishing Corp., 1961

Weiss, Harvey, *Clay, Wood and Wire*, William R. Scott, Inc., 1956

———, *Paper, Ink and Roller*, William R. Scott, Inc., 1958

Design

Christensen, Erwin O., *The Index of American Design*, Macmillan Co., 1959

Downer, Marion, *Discovering Design*, Lothrop, Lee & Shepard Co., Inc., 1947

Randall, R. and Haines, E., *Design in Three Dimensions*, Davis Publications, 1965

Lettering and Commercial Art

Art Directors Club of New York, *44th Annual of Advertising and Editorial Art and Design*, Reinhold Publishing Corp., 1965

Ballinger, Raymond A., *Lettering Art in Modern Use*, Reinhold Publishing Corp., 1965

———, *Layout*, Reinhold Publishing Corp., 1956

Biegeleisen, Jacob I., *The ABC of Lettering*, Harper & Row, Publishers, Inc., 1958

Cartoons and Caricatures

Becker, Stephen, *Comic Art in America*, Simon and Schuster, Inc., 1959

Chase, John, *Today's Cartoon*, The Hauser Press, 1962

Hofmann, Werner, *Caricatures, Leonardo to Picasso*, Crown Publishers, Inc., 1957

Saturday Evening Post (editors), *Feeling Better?*, E. P. Dutton & Co., 1963

Schneider, William H., *Danger! Men Talking*, Random House, Inc., 1965

Thorndyke, Melissa, *My Family and I*, Grosset & Dunlap, Inc., 1964

Art Appreciation

Barr, A. H., Jr., *What Is Modern Painting?*, Museum of Modern Art, 1958

——————, *Masters of Modern Art*, Museum of Modern Art, 1959

Chase, Alice Elizabeth, *Famous Paintings: An Introduction to Art for Young People*, The Platt & Munk Co., Inc., 1962

Cheney, Sheldon, *A New World History of Art*, The Viking Press, 1956

——————, *Story of Modern Art*, The Viking Press, 1958

Holme, Bryan, *Pictures to Live With*, The Viking Press, 1959

Kainz, Luise C. & Riley, O. L., *Exploring Art*, Harcourt, Brace and World, Inc., 1947

Kuh, Katharine, *Art Has Many Faces*, Harper & Row, Publishers, Inc., 1951

Lingstrom, Freda, *The Seeing Eye*, Macmillan Co., 1960

Moore, Lamont, *The First Book of Architecture*, Franklin Watts, Inc., 1961

Rathbun, Mary C. and Hayes, Bartlett H., Jr., *Layman's Guide to Modern Art*, David McKay Co., Inc., 1954

Ruskin, Ariane, *The Pantheon Story of Art for Young People*, Pantheon Books, 1964

Art in the Home

Architectural Record (editors), *A Treasury of Contemporary Houses*, McGraw-Hill Book Co., Inc., 1954

Austin, Ruth E. & Parvis, J. O., *Furnishing Your Home*, Houghton Mifflin Co., 1961

Comstock, Helen, *100 Most Beautiful Rooms in America*, (Studio) The Viking Press, 1965

Ishimoto, Tatsuo and Kiyoko, *The Japanese House: Its Interior and Exterior*, Crown Publishers, Inc., 1963

Moody, Ella, *Decorative Art, Vol. 3*, (Studio) The Viking Press, 1963

Reist, J. A., *Elegant Decorating on a Limited Budget*, Macmillan Co., 1965

Seventeen (editors), *Seventeen Book of Decorating*, David McKay Co., Inc., 1961

Tweed, Katharine, *Finest Rooms by America's Great Decorators*, The Viking Press, 1964

References for Teachers

Barford, George, *Clay in the Classroom*, Davis Publications, Inc., 1963

Barkan, Manuel, *A Foundation for Art Education*, The Ronald Press Co., 1955

Cincinnati Public Schools, *Art Education, Grades 7, 8, 9*, Curriculum Bulletin #50, 1958

Conant, Howard and Randall, Arne, *Art in Education*, Chas. A. Bennett Co., Inc., 1963

D'Amico, Victor, *Creative Teaching in Art*, International Textbook Co., 1953

De Francesco, Italo, *Art Education: Its Means and Ends*, Harper & Row, Publishers, Inc., 1958

Emerson, Sybil, *Design: A Creative Approach*, International Textbook Co., 1953

Kepes, György, *Language of Vision*, Paul Theobald and Co., 1945

Lowenfeld, Viktor and Brittain, W. L., *Creative and Mental Growth*, Macmillan Co., 1964

Meilach, Dona & Hoor, E. T., *Collage and Found Art*, Reinhold Publishing Corp., 1964

Read, Herbert, *Education Through Art*, Pantheon Books, 1958

Reed, Carl, *Early Adolescent Art Education*, Chas. A. Bennett Co., Inc., 1957

Index . . .

0